NORTHERN CYPRUS

NORTHERN CYPRUS

A Traveller's Guide

EILEEN DAVEY

I.B.Tauris Publishers
London · New York

Published in 1993 by
I.B.Tauris & Co Ltd
45 Bloomsbury Square
London WC1A 2HY

175 Fifth Avenue
New York
NY 10010

In the United States of America
and Canada distributed by
St Martin's Press
175 Fifth Avenue
New York
NY 10010

A full CIP record for this book is available from the British Library

Library of Congress Catalog card number: 93-60754
A full CIP record for this book is available from the Library of
Congress

ISBN 1-85043-747-5

The extract on page 20 from Book XXIII of *The Iliad* by Homer
in the translation by W. H. D. Rouse, published by Thomas Nelson
& Sons Ltd in 1938, is reproduced by kind permission of the
publisher.

Typeset in 10/12 Ehrhardt by The Midlands Book Typesetting Co.
Printed and bound in Great Britain by
WBC Ltd, Bridgend, Mid Glamorgan

Contents

———— o ◯ o ————

Author's Note

———— o O o ————

This guide is the kind of visitors' handbook the author has often wished for in an unfamiliar country.

Essentially, it is a collection of in-depth, practical guides, taking the visitor around the most interesting sites. Each chapter has an introduction giving the historical background which sets the monuments in context and peoples them with some of the more colourful characters from the past.

The arrangement is flexible. Each tour guide can be used on its own. On the other hand, the chapters are in chronological order, and so the introductions could be read through as a brief overview of the varied history of Cyprus.

It is offered in the hope that it will add to your understanding and enjoyment of an ancient and fascinating country.

Note on Place Names

———— ○○○ ————

After 1974, all places in North Cyprus were given Turkish names, a fact which obviously complicates any historical narrative.

This guide generally uses the Turkish version, with the old names given in brackets for reference when using pre-1974 maps or literature. There are two exceptions. First, Nicosia, Kyrenia and Famagusta are retained as they are used internationally and are still recognized in North Cyprus. When giving directions involving signposts, both versions are given, for example Lefkoşa (Nicosia), Girne (Kyrenia) and Gazimağusa (Famagusta). Second, prehistoric sites are under the names appearing in the original reports, for example Ayios Epiktitos-Vrysi.

RECOMMENDED MAPS

The local Tourist Map is adequate for route planning.

A better version is the Map of Cyprus (North and South) published by K. Rüstem and Brother, available from their bookshop opposite the Saroy Hotel in Nicosia. Good street maps of the main towns.

The AA/Macmillan Cyprus Travelling Map (available in England) is the only map giving both Turkish and Greek place names, which can be useful. The street map of Nicosia is inadequate.

Maps and Plans

————— o O o —————

Maps and Plans prepared by Chris Sidaway.

Geographical Guide

———— ○ ◯ ○ ————

Sites in the vicinity of:

KYRENIA

Ayios Epiktitos-Vrysi
Karmi-Palealona
Fishponds of Lambousa
Chrysocava
Armenian Monastery
Antiphonitis Monastery
Bellapais
St Hilarion Castle
Buffavento Castle
Haci Ömer Mosque (Lower Lapta)
Seyit Mehmet Ağa Mosque (Upper Lapta)
Hazreti Ömer Mescit

In Kyrenia

Kyrenia Castle
Ağa Cafer Mosque
Ottoman Fountains
Customs House
Harbour Works
British Offices

NICOSIA

Değirmenlik House

Minareliköy Mosque
Arif Paşa Aqueduct

In Nicosia

Selimiye Mosque (St Sophia Cathedral)
Haydarpaşa Mosque (St Catherine's)
Bedestan
Arabahmet Mosque
Yeni Cami Mosque
Derviş Paşa Museum
Mevlevi Derviş Tekke
Büyük Han
Kumarcılar Han
Büyük Haman
Sultan Mahmut II Library
Ottoman Fountains
Georgian Architecture (Victoria Street/S. Salahi Şevket Street)

FAMAGUSTA

Enkomi-Alasia
Tombs of the Kings
Cenotaph of Nicocreon
Salamis – Roman remains and Christian Basilicas
St Barnabas Monastery
İskele (Trikomo) – St James and Panayia Theotokos
Kantara Castle

In Famagusta

Lala Mustafa Paşa Mosque (St Nicholas Cathedral)
St George of the Greeks
SS Peter and Paul
Knights Templar and Knights Hospitaller
Venetian Walls and Gates
Akkule Mescid
Namık Kemal Museum
Cafer Paşa Bath
Canbulat Museum
No. I Railway Engine

GÜZELYURT (MORPHOU)

Myrtou-Pigadhes
Vouni
Soloi
Lefke – Turkish and Georgian Houses
 Piri Paşa Mosque

In Güzelyurt

St Mamas Monastery
No. 3 Railway Engine

KİRPAŞA (THE KARPAS)

Cape Andreas-Kastros
Nitovikla
Ayia Trias
Ayios Philon
Aphendrika
Kanakaria Monastery

Introduction

———— ○○○ ————

Northern Cyprus is a very beautiful country, blessed with an equable climate, where the pine-clad mountains sweep down to the olive groves and picturesque coastline. But it has more more to offer than a perfect setting for a peaceful holiday.

It is a very ancient land, strewn with the relics of the great Mediterranean civilisations. It has had a much livelier and more influential history than a small island might expect. Tucked into the far south-eastern corner of the Mediterranean, only 44 miles from Turkey, 64 miles from Syria, and 211 miles from Egypt, it lies on the frontier between Europe and Asia, between Christianity and Islam.

In AD 985 the Arabic author Shams ad Din, 'Muqaddasi', wrote of Cyprus, 'The island is in the power of whichever nation is overlord in these seas'. He was speaking of the contemporary struggle between the Byzantine Empire and the Arabs, but his words have been equally true during most of the last 3000 years. Cyprus has been fought over and occupied for its strategic military position, for its command of trading routes or for its natural resources, especially copper. At times it has enjoyed wealth and fame out of all proportion to its size; at times it has stagnated as a poor forgotten backwater. But all the great powers left rich traces of their culture, and the story of this colourful, turbulent past can be explored today in the relics which litter the countryside.

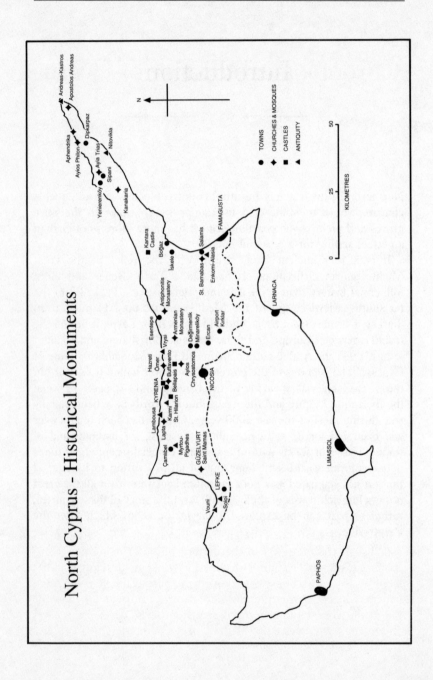

Chronological History of Cyprus

PREHISTORIC CYPRUS

Pre-7000 Paleolithic Age.   One site, at Aetokremnos.
7000–3900 BC Neolithic Age.   Two distinct Neolithic cultures, the Aceramic and the Late Neolithic, were separated by an unexplained gap of 1500 years.
3900–2500 BC Chalcolithic Age.   Developed as an interim stage between the Stone and Bronze Ages.

BRONZE AGE CYPRUS

2500–1900 BC Early Bronze Age.   No settlements have been excavated but rich grave goods found in the cemeteries of Philea and Vounous.
1900–1600 BC Middle Bronze Age.   Cyprus established firm trading links with Syria, Asia Minor and Egypt. Tablets found in Egypt and Syria refer to 'Alashiya' as a copper-bearing country. Lapithos on the north coast became the most important city.
1600–1050 BC Late Bronze Age.   In Cyprus as on the mainland this was a period of great prosperity, reaching its height between 1400 BC and 1250 BC. Foreign trade increased. The Mycenaeans established trading posts in the eastern ports, bringing new techniques in pottery. Lapithos declined as Enkomi developed into a major trading and copper-working city. Around 1200 BC there was a general collapse of the splendid Late Bronze culture, marked by the fall of the Hittite Empire, the destruction of the Mycenaean cities and the appearance around 1190 BC of the marauding Sea Peoples. Enkomi was devastated and eventually abandoned for Salamis.

ARCHAIC CYPRUS

1050–325 BC Iron Age. After the devastation which destroyed the Late Bronze cities, a Dark Age fell on the Eastern Mediterranean. Little is known of the next 200 years. An influx of displaced refugees, mostly Achaeans from the Aegean, brought their language and culture and mingled with the native Cypriots. New towns grew up, near the old cities, notably Salamis and Lapta. Cyprus emerged from the Dark Age in the eighth century, organized into city kingdoms and largely Greek-speaking. Prosperity built up, based on renewed trade links, encouraged by Phoenician settlements, e.g. Kition. The royal tombs of the kings of Salamis are witness to the cosmopolitan wealth and culture of the eighth and seventh centuries.

708 BC The city kings paid tribute to Sargon II of Assyria.

570 BC Cyprus came under suzerainty of Egypt.

PERSIAN CYPRUS

545 BC Cypriot kings submitted to Cyrus, King of Persia.

499 BC Most Cypriot kingdoms joined the unsuccessful revolt of the Greek Ionian cities against Persia.

450 BC Cimon of Athens led an expedition to recover Cyprus from the Persians, with only short-lived success.

435–374 BC Evagoras of Salamis reclaimed his throne from a Phoenician usurper, then embarked on an ambitious attempt to unite the kingdoms (often against their own wishes). He was defeated in 381 BC, but allowed to remain king of Salamis. An ardent enthusiast for Hellenic culture, he did much to reinforce the ties with the Greek mainland.

HELLENISTIC CYPRUS

330 BC Cypriot city states joined Alexander the Great.

323 BC Death of Alexander. Two of his generals, Antigonus and Ptolemy of Egypt, fought over Cyprus with varying fortunes.

311 BC Death of Nicocreon of Salamis.

294 BC Ptolemy established his control and Cyprus became part of the Egyptian empire for nearly 300 years. Under the Ptolemies, the island was prosperous but lost much of its identity. The ancient city kingdoms disappeared. Cyprus was still part of the Hellenic world, but looked to Alexandria rather than Athens.

336 BC Zeno, the founder of the Stoic philosophy, was born in Kition.

ROMAN CYPRUS

58 BC Cyprus was annexed by Rome, the rising Mediterranean power.

22 BC Cyprus made a senatorial province, divided into four administrative districts, Paphos, Salamis, Amathus and Lapethos. Paphos was the capital but Salamis the richest city, with a mixed population of Greek Cypriots, Romans and Jews which might have reached 350,000. The emperors built lavishly in Salamis, Soloi, Paphos and other cities, particularly after the severe earthquakes in AD 77. Roads, harbours, aqueducts, theatres, temples, market-places and public baths obliterated much of the Hellenic cities.

45 Barnabas and Saul sailed from Antioch to Salamis, crossed the island and converted the proconsul, Sergius Paulus, at Paphos. Cyprus became the first country to have a Christian ruler. Barnabas was later martyred at Salamis.

115 The Cypriot Jews revolted against Rome, and were expelled from the island. But under the Pax Romana Cyprus flourished. The Cypriots were already acquiring the reputation for wealth, luxury and immorality which dogged them through the Middle Ages.

325 Constantine the Great, having made Christianity the State religion, convened the Council of Nicaea to settle internal doctrinal disputes. Three Cypriot bishops were present.

332 and 342 saw two devastating earthquakes. Salamis, which was also submerged by a tidal wave, was rebuilt by the Emperor Constantius II (337–61), who renamed it Constantia.

395 The Roman Empire finally split into two. Cyprus became part of the Eastern Roman Empire, governed from Constantine I's new capital, Constantinople (Byzantium).

BYZANTINE CYPRUS

For the next 800 years, Cyprus was part of the Byzantine Empire, Greek in language and Orthodox Christian in religion. The first two centuries under the new regime continued to be peaceful and prosperous.

478 Archbishop Anthemias fought off an attempted takeover of the Cypriot Church by the See of Antioch, with the help of a timely dream.

647 Inspired by Islam, the Arabs had already taken Egypt and the Levant. They now raided Cyprus and sacked Salamis-Constantia.

688 Treaty between the Emperor Justinian II and the Arabs effectively established a condominium in Cyprus, the revenues to be divided between the signatories.

965 The Emperor Nicephoros Phocas expelled the Arabs and reimposed Byzantine rule. New, smaller churches with frescoes and domes replaced the ruins of the great basilicas. The first castles were built on the northern range.

1184 Isaac Comnenos, a cadet of the imperial family, declared himself Emperor of Cyprus. His rule was oppressive and brutal, but lasted only seven years.

1187 The Seljuk Turks captured Jerusalem.

1191 Richard I of England, on his way to the Third Crusade, deposed Isaac and sold the island to the Knights Templar for 100,000 bezants. They were unable to control the Cypriots and asked Richard to take it back. He then sold it to Guy de Lusignan as compensation for the loss of his kingdom of Jersualem.

LUSIGNAN CYPRUS 1192–1489

The next 300 years were the most spectacular in the history of Cyprus. Under the Lusignans the island acquired immense wealth and a European reputation for exotic (if decadent) splendour. This was largely confined to the Latin nobles, who remained aloof from the native Greek Orthodox peasants. In the early years of the dynasty, the Crusades consumed much energy and wealth and brought unwelcome foreign interference. Internally there were periodic upheavals caused by the frequent minorities. Lusignan kings, being men of action, tended to die young. The family of d'Ibelin, much intermarried with the royal family, were often regents and gained great power, especially John d'Ibelin, known as the Old Lord of Beirut, who built Kyrenia Castle and refortified St Hilarion.

1218 The death of Hugh I on Crusade left an heir of nine months, Henry I. His minority was marked by quarrels between the co-regents, the Queen Mother and Philip and John d'Ibelin, complicated by the intervention of the Holy Roman Emperor, Frederick II, while on Crusade. Kyrenia and St Hilarion castles both suffered long sieges.

1244 The Crusaders finally lost Jerusalem.

1260 The Bulla Cypria brought the Orthodox Church in Cyprus under the Roman. The four Orthodox Bishops gave an oath of obedience to the Latin Archbishop, and were banished to villages away from their cathedrals; all tithes went to the Roman Clergy.

1267   The accession of Hugh III marked the beginning of the most splendid years of the Lusignan dynasty. He was soldier, scholar, experienced administrator and patron of the arts. To him Thomas Aquinas dedicated his great work *De Regimine Principum*.

1291   Acre, the last stronghold of the Latins in the Levant, fell to the Mamelukes. Acre had been the commercial entrepot between East and West; all the great mercantile cities traded within its walls. They now fled to Famagusta, which rapidly became the wealthiest port in Europe. The Military Orders, the Hospitallers and the Knights Templar, also took refuge in Cyprus until the Templars were dissolved for heresy and the Hospitallers found new headquarters in Rhodes.

1324–59 Hugh IV. 1359–69 Peter I.   Supported by the immense wealth generated in Famagusta, the Cypriot court dazzled Europe. Even the Black Death, which decimated Cyprus in 1349, was only a temporary setback (the royal family took refuge in St Hilarion).

Peter I, charismatic but impractical, made extensive tours through Europe trying to revive the crusading spirit. He managed to raise forces which he led to the capture and sack of Alexandria. His failure to arouse further support in Europe for his lifelong dream, the re-establishment of the kingdom of Jersualem, brought out an inherent instability. On his return to Cyprus, an accusation against his queen, Eleanor of Aragon, provoked him to such brutal retaliation that he was assassinated by his nobles.

1369   The rapid decline of the Lusignans began at the coronation of his young son, Peter II. Several Genoese were killed after a scuffle with the Venetians over precedence. Genoa retaliated by sending an army which forced Cyprus to cede Famagusta to Genoa. With Famagusta went much of the Lusignans' wealth, while the presence of Genoese troops in Famagusta was a constant threat.

1398   Janus, born while his father was in captivity in Genoa, reigned for 34 disastrous years. In 1426 the Mamelukes inflicted a terrible defeat on his forces at Khirokitia. Janus was taken prisoner to Egypt and released only in return for a ruinous ransom, the promise of an annual tribute and his accepting the sultan as overlord. The proud Lusignan dynasty was reduced to a vassal of Egypt.

1432–58   His son John was married to Helena, a Greek princess, who tried to revive the Orthodox Church in Cyprus.

1458–60   John's daughter, Charlotte, succeeded, backed by the nobility. Her illegitimate brother James went to Cairo to get support from the sultan. With the help of an Egyptian fleet, James took the island and besieged Charlotte's supporters in Kyrenia Castle for three years. She fled to Rome.

1460–73 James was crowned and recaptured Famagusta from the Genoese. But he made the fatal mistake of marrying Caterina Cornaro of Venice. A year later James was dead; his posthumous son lived only a year.

1474–89 Caterina Cornaro, daughter of Venice, was queen. All her principal officers were Venetian; she did as she was told. But she was still young enough to remarry and in 1489 Venice persuaded her to abdicate. The Lusignan dynasty had finally ended.

THE VENETIAN OCCUPATION 1489–1571

Venice had triumphed over Genoa and the Lusignans, but its hold on Cyprus was far from secure. The Ottoman Turks had been steadily increasing their power in the eastern Mediterranean. In 1453 the Eastern Roman Empire fell to the Turks when the last emperor died fighting on the walls of Constantinople. In 1522 Rhodes was captured from the Hospitallers. After Syria and Egypt were taken by the Turks from the Mamelukes, Venice sent the annual tribute due from the island not to Cairo but to Constantinople, thus recognizing the Ottoman claim to the suzerainty of Cyprus.

So Venice always regarded Cyprus as a military outpost which would one day have to be defended against the Turk. Kyrenia Castle was rebuilt and Nicosia and Famagusta strongly fortified.

1570–71 The blow finally fell. A strong force of Turks overran the island with the exception of Nicosia, Kyrenia and Famagusta. Nicosia fell in September 1570 and Kyrenia surrendered. In August 1571, Famagusta was taken after a courageous resistance. For the next 300 years Cyprus was a Turkish dependency. Europe was shocked but did nothing to help. The discovery of a sea route to the East around the Cape of Good Hope had given control of trade to the maritime nations of Western Europe. Cyprus became an obscure backwater.

OTTOMAN CYPRUS 1571–1878

Cyprus at first welcomed the Turks, who suppressed the hated Latin Church and abolished the feudal system. The Orthodox Church was encouraged; the Ottomans were tolerant. They administered their domains under the *millet* system, which classified subject peoples by religion rather than race, and made use of the various religious leaders. Turkish settlers were given land and eventually made up a third of the population.

But the administration was inefficient. The right to collect taxes was farmed out to the highest bidder, who naturally raised as much as possible. Drought, locusts, famine and plague and emigration decimated the population. From 1660 the bishops gradually took over control from the inefficient pashas sent from the mainland and became virtual rulers, until the Greek revolt against the Ottomans in 1821 led to the execution of the Orthodox Patriarch in Constantinople and a general massacre of Christians in Cyprus.

1839 The sultan issued the 'Khatt-i-Sherif', a decree reforming the medieval administration of the Porte on modern lines. The reforms secured equality for all Ottoman subjects, remodelled the administration and promised security of life and property. Tax-farming was abolished, and officials from the governor down received fixed salaries. Although the reforms were not wholly enforced, and little of the revenue was spent on public works, the condition of Cyprus improved during the nineteenth century.

1869 The opening of the Suez Canal redirected maritime trade through the eastern Mediterranean. After three centuries of obscurity, Cyprus regained strategic importance.

1878 The Anglo-Turkish Convention leased Cyprus to Britain in return for an annual tribute and mutual support against the Russians.

BRITISH ADMINISTRATION 1878–1960

Though chronically short of money, the administration surveyed the island, introduced a postal system and a police force, constructed roads and harbours, conducted an anti-locust campaign and improved health by eliminating malaria.

1914 Turkey supported the Germans in the First World War. Britain retaliated by annexing Cyprus.

1925 Cyprus became a Crown Colony.

1931 Government House was burned down during rioting for independence.

After the Second World War there was increased agitation for independence. EOKA began guerrilla warfare under Grivas. EOKA wanted Enosis, union with Greece. There were about 500 deaths, some EOKA members were executed and Archbishop Makarios, playing his historic role as political as well as religious leader of his flock, was exiled.

1959 Makarios returned, having officially abandoned Enosis.

INDEPENDENCE

1960 The independent Republic of Cyprus was established by the London Accord, signed by Britain, Greece and Turkey. Makarios became the first president. A complicated system of checks and balances failed to protect the Turkish minority.

1963 Attacks on Turkish communities brought in UN troops to police the Green Line drawn across Nicosia.

1971 Grivas reactivated EOKA B without the support of Makarios and embarked on a campaign of terrorism against Turks and moderate Greeks.

1974 Grivas died and Makarios was re-elected. His attempt to get mainland Greek troops withdrawn from the island led to a coup d'état organized by the Greek officers, encouraged by the Colonels' regime in Athens. Makarios was deposed and fled. Turkey cited their obligation under the Treaty of Guarantee and sent over troops. The Turkish army advanced to the present 'Attila Line'. Makarios returned to the south.

1975 The Turkish Federal State was set up under Rauf Denktaş. The population was relocated under UN supervision; 120,000 Greeks went to the south and 65,000 Turks to the north.

1983 Creation of the Turkish Republic of North Cyprus. Only Turkey and Nakhichevan have so far recognized the independent republic. The partition line continues to be patrolled by UN troops. So far attempts at negotiation have failed to find a solution.

CHAPTER ONE

Stone Age Villages and Bronze Age Cities

———————— o ◯ o ————————

ARCHEOLOGY IN CYPRUS

Cyprus is strewn with ancient cities, settlements and cemeteries, but serious archeological appraisal began surprisingly late, the first scientific expedition being in 1927.

Many early sites were destroyed by earthquake and fire. From the Middle Ages, stone-robbers found the battered remains convenient sources of dressed stone, while tomb-robbers supplemented meagre peasant livings by occasional forays underground. Under British rule stone-robbing supplied the quays of Port Said and the Suez Canal. Unofficial excavation continues today on well-known sites like Ayia Irini and Vounous, aided by the unfortunate invention of the metal detector.

Pious medieval travellers, well-read in the Bible and the classics, explored with enthusiasm the sites of Teucer's Salamis and the miracle of St Barnabas, and were not above buying their souvenirs from the grave-robbers. In the early nineteenth century, the chance discovery of the Cypriot syllabic script aroused the interest of European scholars, who devoted their research to deciphering the inscriptions. Then in the second half of the century the gentlemanly foreign amateurs appeared. Diplomats with a taste for the past, encouraged by Schliemann's successes at Troy, vied with each other in excavating and exporting vast quantities of antiquities which furnished the major museums of the West. The most remarkable was General Luigi Palma di Cesnola, appointed US and Russian consul in Cyprus from 1865 to 1877, who sold his collection to the New York Metropolitan Museum. More damage was done to the sites by these enthusiasts than by centuries of looting by peasants.

1

In 1878 the British administration restricted unofficial excavation. The Cyprus Museum was established in 1883. Several German and British expeditions carried out more or less haphazard excavations. But serious scientific archeology began in Cyprus with the Swedish expeditions of 1927 to 1931. Their meticulous excavation techniques and classification of finds are the basis of Cypriot archeology.

After the establishment of the Department of Antiquities in 1934, Cypriot excavations became very popular, particularly on Neolithic and Bronze Age sites, and in the great cities such as Salamis and Soloi. Since 1974, the partition of the island has inevitably hampered research.

Many excavations in North Cyprus are either difficult of access or unrewarding for the lay visitor. The most interesting sites are described in detail, against the historical background which explains and illuminates them. Together they illustrate a complete cross-section of the early history of Cyprus.

Culture	Dates	Sites
Paleolithic	–7000 BC	One Paleolithic site has been tentatively identified
Neolithic		
Aceramic	7000–6000 BC	Cape Andreas-Kastros
Late Neolithic	4500–3900 BC	Ayios Epiktitos-Vrysi
Chalcolithic	3900–2500 BC	Ambelikou
Bronze Age		
Early	2500–1900 BC	Vounous
Middle	1900–1650 BC	Karmi. Nitovikla
Late	1650–1050 BC	Enkomi. Myrtou-Pigadhes

The human occupation of Cyprus is surprisingly recent, considering there are well-documented Old Stone Age settlements in neighbouring Anatolia. Only one possible Paleolithic site has so far been discovered in Cyprus.

The Neolithic culture is in two distinct phases, separated by an unexplained gap of 1500 years. The main difference is the introduction of pottery in Late Neolithic.

ACERAMIC 7000–6000 BC

The small villages were very thinly scattered around the north and south coasts. The inhabitants were a short-headed people, whose origin is unknown. It is possible they came from the Syrian coast, visible from eastern Cyprus; their burial customs show many similarities with contemporary graves in the Levant. Ornaments of carnelian and tools made of obsidian, a volcanic glass not found in Cyprus, must have come from the mainland and could have been brought over by the original settlers. Certainly Neolithic man had the technical ability to cross such a narrow body of water.

The Aceramic people built circular one-roomed huts, or *tholoi*, grouped closely together in permanent settlements. The bottom half was solidly constructed of boulders or stones, topped by sun-dried brick. The flat roofs were supported on rafters. They had no knowledge of pottery, but made finely finished and decorated stone vessels with spouts and handles. They had spindles and bone needles, so they wove cloth, probably wool. Flint weapons were not as advanced as on the mainland; archeologists have found no javelin points and few arrow heads. Figurines in clay and stone may have been idols. They practised mixed farming, keeping sheep and goats and growing barley which they harvested with flint sickles and ground with querns and grinders made from boulders. They supplemented their diet by hunting.

Cape Andreas-Kastros

This, one of the earliest Neolithic settlements, was excavated by a French mission led by A. LeBrun in 1970–73. It is situated on the extreme tip of the Kirpaşa (Karpas) peninsula, on a sheltered southern-facing shelf half-way up a steep promontory jutting out into the sea. The hut circles can be seen from across the little bay. The position strengthens the probability that the original settlers came from the Levant. The site is easily defensible and protects an anchorage for fishing boats.

The houses are the usual circular huts, though the shape is sometimes distorted by the stony outcrops. The floors are beaten earth, with a central hearth, and mud or stone platforms against the walls. The construction is of rubble, less solid than in, for example, Khirokitia (an extensive site on the southern coast), but it was a permanent and well-organized settlement. There are signs of the usual agricultural/hunting pursuits, here supplemented by fishing. Quantities of lentils, peas, olives, nuts and figs were found in the houses, together with fishing implements, fish bones and shells.

The burial rites followed the same pattern as the other Aceramic communities. The dead were venerated and appeased. They were buried in shallow pits in a foetal position with the knees against the chest, the graves usually inside the huts underneath the floor. Large stones were often placed on the chest of the corpse, showing some anxiety about its activities in an afterlife. Grave goods include broken stone bowls and necklaces and pins of cornelian and shell.

LATE NEOLITHIC 4500–3900 BC

About 6000 BC, this early culture disappeared, seemingly as a natural decline. Between 6000 and 4500 BC, there are few signs of human habitation. Around 4500 BC a new and distinctly different culture appears. The houses show a variety of shapes, notably rectangular with rounded corners, the dead are buried away from the houses in pits, and there are many more villages. The people made excellent decorated pottery. The bowls and jugs from all sites are similar in shape, but there is a difference in decoration between the south and the north. The southern potters used the distinctive combed techniques while the north went in for strongly painted designs.

Ayios Epiktitos-Vrysi

An interesting and important site to the east of Kyrenia along the coast road. Turn off the main road at the Acapulco sign, drive through the complex and out on the headland to the east of the bay. It can also be approached from the Eight Mile Beach.

The excavation was carried out by Glasgow University in 1969–73. The earliest estimated date is 4660 BC, which puts it at the very beginning of the new wave of settlers. Vrysi is a narrow promontory surrounded on three sides by the sea, ideally situated for defence. The new arrivals do not seem to have had any opposition, however. The headland was at first protected by a large ditch 7 m. wide by 4 m. deep, but this was soon abandoned and houses built outside it as the settlement expanded. There was fertile, well-watered agricultural land nearby.

The houses are very irregular, fitting into the rocky uneven ground.

Where possible the typical rectangle with rounded corners appears. The first huts were in hollows cut down into the living rock; stone walls lined the hollows, topped by mud brick. These thin walls were plastered on the inside. Because the houses were frequently rebuilt on the same foundations, the level of the rooms, originally sunken, gradually rose. The excavation has gone down to the bedrock, leaving some of the walls exposed to the height of 3 m. The one-roomed houses were sometimes divided by wooden beams; they had circular platform hearths set to one side and wall benches. The flat roofs were covered with reeds laid across timbers. They are arranged in groups separated by very narrow passages.

These people were farmers who cultivated wheat, barley, lentils, olives and vines and reared sheep, goats and possibly pigs. They hunted deer and collected seafood. They manufactured stone and bone implements and practised basketry and weaving, leaving many spindle whorls and bone needles. Their pottery was advanced, including large bottles and bowls. A whitish slip was prepared by covering the pot with a thin solution of clay before firing. On this were painted bold designs in red or brown, based on combinations of circles and dashes. Later artists painted parallel rows of ripples which show affinity with the combed decoration popular in the south.

The dead were buried outside the houses, in the foetal position. There is a hint of religious practices in the two stone pillars found in one house, which had been covered with plaiting; one was phallic in shape.

Late Neolithic Cyprus developed peacefully for almost a thousand years. The population grew and spread over most of the east of the island. Vrysi flourished until it was abandoned suddenly about 3800 BC. Many other sites were left at about the same time, possibly as the result of an earthquake.

(Vrysi has been exposed for 20 years and is showing serious signs of deterioration. It is difficult to preserve prehistoric sites built of rubble and mud; the tall, thin walls dividing the houses at Vrysi are particularly susceptible to erosion. At Khirokitia, a Neolithic site on the south coast, the mud between the stones has been replaced by mud-coloured cement, which is efficient but not wholly acceptable. There is a suggestion that Vrysi could be infilled to within a few feet of the top, thus preserving a very important Neolithic site for future research. It is also to be hoped that the Department of Antiquities can find the resources from their limited budget to carry out the projected extension to Kyrenia Castle Museum to display some of the artefacts from Vrysi, at present in store.)

CHALCOLITHIC 3900–2500 BC

Chalcolithic means literally copper/stone and is the name given to the interim period between the Stone and Bronze Ages when a few metal objects are found side by side with Stone Age technology. Metal-working was in the native copper, unalloyed by the additions of arsenic or tin which were to produce the harder bronze. New areas were settled along the south-west coast and the flanks of the Kyrenia Mountains. The pottery was imaginative and lively. The most extraordinary development was in religion, which evolved from the Neolithic veneration of the dead to a form of fertility worship. Large numbers of female figures with extended arms have been found. These small cruciform idols are usually carved in a standard pattern out of picrolite and often pierced to hang as pendants or necklaces. The goddess was to reappear in Cypriot religion for many centuries, down to the cult of Aphrodite.

THE BRONZE AGE 2500–1050 BC

The discovery of metal – the use of bronze instead of laboriously chipped and ground stone – was one of the major technological advances. The effect on Cyprus was particularly shattering. For Cyprus possessed vast reserves of copper, the essential raw material. The very name Cyprus is connected with the word for copper. The island was torn out of its peacefully productive Stone Age isolation. Copper meant trade, wealth, sophistication – and war. There was internal tension between the west, which controlled the mines and the east, which had the arable land. More significantly, Cyprus was to become a valuable pawn in the power struggles of the eastern Mediterranean.

EARLY BRONZE AGE 2500–1900 BC

Bronze Age culture developed first in north-west Cyprus around Güzelyurt (Morphou) Bay, and spread slowly through the island, the old ways persisting longest in the south. It was probably an indigenous development but may have been influenced by refugees from western Anatolia, where a well-established Bronze Age culture was disrupted by a widespread disaster *c.* 2500 BC.

No settlement has been excavated. Fortunately for our knowledge of the period, the dead were now buried in large cemeteries outside the villages and provided with rich and varied grave goods. These yield ample evidence of the wealth, sophistication and trade links of the new era. Two large graveyards have been excavated in North Cyprus, at Vounous and Lapethos.

Vounous

The extensively excavated cemetery of Vounous lies on the slope of a hill a few miles south of Bellapais. It is difficult of access but has to be included because of the unparalleled importance of the finds. The pottery, mainly Red Polished, is complex and imaginative in shape and decoration, sometimes with birds and animals perched around the rim of bowls. Bull motifs show that cattle have at last been introduced. (The skeleton of a horse was found at Lapethos.) Foreign imports include a jug from Syria, daggers from Minoan Crete and beads from Egypt. There are useful terracotta models of contemporary scenes; one shows pairs of oxen drawing ploughs of a type still in use. Models of open-air sanctuaries depict men and women making offerings to figures wearing bull masks and holding snakes, symbols of fertility and the underworld. Female idols in red terracotta shaped as flat planks have details picked out by white lines – arms crossed on the breast, long decorated skirts, wavy hair held in place with headbands, and many necklaces. Many tombs contained daggers but there is no evidence of war.

MIDDLE BRONZE AGE 1900–1650 BC

This short period of transition shows four main developments:

1. An increase in cultural and trading contacts with Syria, Palestine and Egypt – even Crete. Cypriot pottery appears on the mainland. Copper was exported in growing quantities. References to 'Alashiya' as a copper-producing island appear in Near Eastern tablets as early as the eighteenth century BC. 'Alashiya' has been fairly conclusively identified with Cyprus.

2. A shift in settlement patterns in the north of the island. Vounous declined in favour of new semi-urban townships in the east.

3. Growing tension between the north-west, which controlled the copper mines, and the north-east, which had the arable land and the nearest ports to the Levant. A chain of inland fortresses was built to provide refuges. Cyprus was also affected by the general instability in the Levant, where the barbarian Hyksos – 'the Princes from foreign lands' – were established in the Nile Delta, a constant threat to Egypt and her neighbours. More forts were built on the coast of Northern Cyprus, possibly for protection, though the south remained peaceful.

4. The introduction of White Painted Pottery. The distinct separation between east and west shows in the differences in the red painted decoration – linear in the east, geometric in the west. The styles are debased, except in the peaceful south which carried serenely on producing elegant Red Polished in an unbroken Chalcolithic tradition.

Karmi (Palealona)

A small but important cemetery. On the coast road west out of Kyrenia, at Karaoğlanoğlu turn left on the road to Karaman (Karmi). Before entering the village, take the secondary road to the left. Less than one kilometre, there is a layby on the left leading to a footpath which runs along the western edge of a steep valley. A very short walk leads to the cemetery.

Palealona was excavated in 1961 by an Australian expedition. The area of the necropolis is limited by a steep rise on the west and a deep ravine to the east. It was in use during the Early and Middle Bronze Ages (2500–1650 BC).

The graves are in the Bronze Age tradition – chamber tombs excavated from solid rock. A steep stepped *dromos*, or entrance passage, leads to the burial chamber, which is entered through a small opening, the *stomion*. This was sealed by a large stone; many are still lying in the graves near the openings. Two or three chambers lead off most of the entrance passages. Because of the restricted area, the tombs are closely grouped, some lying underneath later chambers.

The most interesting finds were made in the centre of the complex, in the graves marked T6 and T11. On the right wall of the *dromos* in T6, is carved an outline relief of a human figure about 1 m. high. This carving is the earliest known funerary stele in Cyprus; it was probably copied from an Egyptian tomb. The entrance to the burial chamber is higher than usual and has rudimentary carving indicating columns and a lintel. This tomb is so important that the

ABOVE Ayios Epiktitos (Vrysi), a site dating from the Late Neolithic period, *c* 4600 BC. These houses were built up inside hollows dug 30 feet into the cliff-top. Vrysi flourished, but was abandoned around 3800 BC, possibly as the result of an earthquake.

RIGHT Myrtou-Pigadhes is the site of a Late Bronze Age (1650–1050 BC) shrine; it was once part of a large settlement, but now stands isolated. The altar with its 'Horns of Consecration' has been reconstructed from the original worked limestone blocks, twelve of which were found in their original position. Bulls and horns were cult symbols in Cyprus from the Early Bronze Age, and horns of consecration topping altars have been found from Knossos to Hittite Boghazköy.

LEFT The mysterious palace of Vouni was built around 500 BC on a hill commanding magnificent views of the Güzelyurt Bay. Built at a time when the Cypriot kingdoms were torn between Greek and Persian factions, there is no known record of who occupied the palace. This windlass (winch) stands over the main water cistern. The central carving, depicting the face of a goddess, was never completed – possibly brought to halt when fire destroyed the palace around 380 BC.

BELOW The royal tombs of Salamis were built by the Archaic rulers of Salamis around 800–600 BC. Tomb 50 was turned into a Roman chapel, known as the Prison of St Catherine after a legendary martyr. Recent excavation uncovered the skeletons of two yoked horses (now under the glass cover) sacrificed at the time of the original burial.

ABOVE An amphora recovered from the merchant ship which sank a mile outside Kyrenia harbour around 306 BC. Today a special museum in Kyrenia Castle houses the cargo and the hull – the oldest ever raised from the sea-bed.

ABOVE RIGHT The Roman public latrines off the exercise ground at Salamis. Forty-four seats are arranged in a semi-circle. Water flowed along a trough in front of the seats and ran into a drainage channel underneath.

RIGHT The east portico at Salamis.

The mosaics in Soloi Basilico. ABOVE LEFT Mosaic from the first period; BELOW LEFT and ABOVE RIGHT From the second period; BELOW RIGHT From the third period.

The Chrysocava, a series of chapels
and refuges cut into the walls of
the old Roman stone quarries, dates
back to the earliest days of Cypriot
Christianity.

The Churches of İskele (Trikomo)

LEFT The Church of St James, one of the smallest and most attractive of the Greek Orthodox churches.

BELOW Panayia Theotokos, formerly the main church of İskele. It was built in the twelfth century as a Byzantine church, enlarged in the fifteenth century, and is now maintained as an icon museum. It contains excellent frescoes from the twelfth and fifteenth centuries.

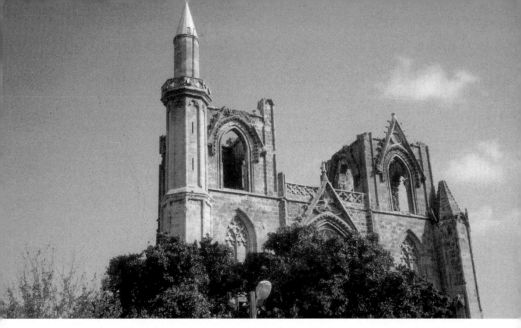

ABOVE St Nicholas, the Lusignan cathedral in Famagusta. Here the Lusignans were crowned kings of Jerusalem.

BELOW Built in the fourteenth century to rival St Nicholas, St George of the Greeks in Famagusta was one of the largest Orthodox cathedrals anywhere and was sited next to the earlier Byzantine church. The architecture in this case is Gothic rather than Orthodox.

The plaque outside the Church of St Mamas, Güzelyurt (Morphou) shows the saint on a lion, holding a lamb. Mamas, a well-known hermit, was arrested for non-payment of taxes. On the way to the governor he rescued a lamb from a lion, then rode the lion into court. The governor remitted his taxes.

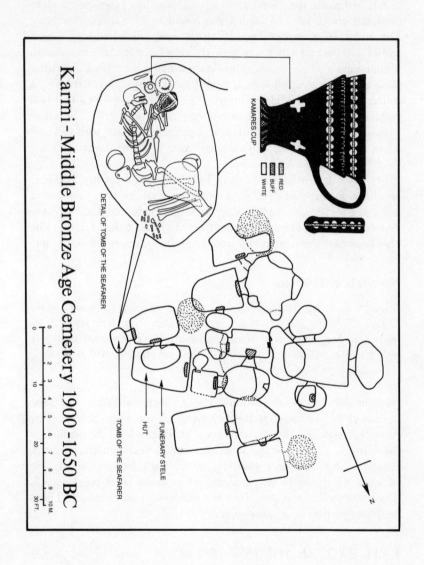

Karmi - Middle Bronze Age Cemetery 1900 - 1650 BC

DETAIL OF TOMB OF THE SEAFARER

KAMARES CUP

RED
BUFF
WHITE

TOMB OF THE SEAFARER

HUT

FUNERARY STELE

0 1 2 3 4 5 6 7 8 9 10 M.
0 10 20 30 FT.

N

University of Sydney paid for the erection of the hut which now protects T6.

While digging the foundations of the hut, the expedition had to clear the *dromos* of T11, which was found to have three chambers: 11A under the *dromos* of T6, 11C to the west which had been looted and 11B to the east which was opened on the last day of the expedition. It contained a single burial. The skeleton had a blue bead under the skull and was surrounded by a large bronze dagger, a small knife, a collection of typical Middle Bronze White Painted and Red Polished pottery – and an imported Kamares ware cup from Crete. This small Minoan object, beautifully made and painted in black with red and white decoration inside and out, has been very important in dating the Middle Bronze Age in Cyprus.

Professor James Stewart called T11B the Tomb of the Seafarer, on the romantic but feasible assumption that its occupant was a sailor serving on the trading ships between Syria and Lapithos, the important Middle Bronze Age port on the coast below Karmi. The blue bead and the Cretan cup would have been treasured souvenirs.

Nitovikla c. 1600 BC

Nitovikla is a large fortress built on a low hill near the south coast of the Karpas. Take the main road to Ziyamet (Leonarisso), turn right at the crossroads, past Kanakaria Monastery, to Kuruova (Korovia) then turn right down to the coast. A four-wheel-drive vehicle is needed to negotiate the rudimentary tracks.

Built at the end of the Middle Bronze Age, Nitovikla was soon destroyed but restored at the beginning of the Late Bronze. The Anatolian style recalls the fortresses at Boghazköy, the capital of the Hittites. Massive stone walls surround a rectangular courtyard. Barracks built around the inside of the walls had flat roofs with parapets which served as platforms for lookouts or to repel assault. The one entrance was protected by squat towers on each side. There were similar towers at two corners.

LATE BRONZE AGE 1650–1050 BC

In the Late Bronze Age, Cyprus finally became involved in the power struggles in the eastern Mediterranean. Her prosperity, though soundly based on copper and trade, was always at the mercy of external forces.

During the first 400 years, relatively stable conditions favoured expansion and wealth. Three great powers controlled the region. The Egyptians finally expelled the Hyksos from the Nile Delta and the powerful Theban Pharaohs of the New Kingdom enforced peace to the south. The great Hittite Empire, stretching from Anatolia to the Euphrates, maintained a precarious balance in the Levant, largely through its sophisticated diplomacy. In the Aegean, the Mycenaean warrior kings of the Heroic Age controlled the Peleponnese and expanded to the islands and the coast of Asia Minor. After the destruction of Knossus *c.* 1400 BC, they took control of Crete and the extensive Minoan trade routes. This brought them into contact with Cyprus, which was on their trade route to Syria. They established trading communities in the existing south-eastern ports, especially Enkomi. The Bronze Age reached its height in the fourteenth and thirteenth centuries with elaborate palace-based bureaucracies controlling trade and industrial production, and wealthy cosmopolitan cities. Though no such 'palaces' have been uncovered in Cyprus, the island developed its own sophisticated urban communities.

The end came with dramatic suddenness. If the Trojan expedition has any basis in historical fact, it would have been the last exploit of the Achaean dynasties. By *c.* 1200 BC all the great Mycenaean cities except Athens had been destroyed by fire, sword or earthquake. The proud Hittite Empire collapsed after its capital at Boghazköy was destroyed *c.* 1180 BC, and almost disappeared from history, The dreaded Sea Peoples appeared – large bands of seaborne warriors, composed of migrants, pirates and displaced Mycenaeans, who raided through Asia Minor, Syria and Palestine, burning the great cities and overturning kingdoms. Their great land and sea raid was only halted at the Nile Delta, where the Pharaoh defeated the Sea Peoples in two pitched battles in 1210 and 1186 BC.

From the Peleponnese to the Nile, Bronze Age civilization collapsed in flames and tumult. Cyprus did not escape.

Enkomi-Alasia 1550–1050 BC

It lies 8 km. north of Famagusta by the side of the main road and is well signposted.

It was first thought to be a cemetery. The tombs were a popular target of local grave-robbers and of foreign expeditions in 1896, 1913 and 1930. In 1934, C. F. A. Schaeffer discovered that it was not a necropolis after all but the site of a large city. The 'graves' were in fact in the courtyards of houses.

The region around the Bay of Salamis is exceptionally favoured. Backed by the fertile Mesarya (Mesaoria) plain, provided with natural harbours, and within a hundred miles of the Syro-Palestine coast, it is the obvious place for an entrepot linking West and East. Enkomi, Salamis and Famagusta have all been the greatest Cypriot ports of their day. The name 'Alashiya' appears frequently in the tablets of the Near East, referring to a copper-producing town or country. Today it is generally taken to mean Cyprus. In 1952, 'Alasia' was added to Enkomi as the capital, though some scholars dispute this. Correspondence on clay tablets between Akhnaten of Egypt and the king of 'Alashiya', in which he refers to the Pharaoh as his 'brother', discusses the exchange of gifts and apologizes for the late delivery of the copper ingots due as tribute. The last tablets written before Ugarit was destroyed were to the king of 'Alashiya' asking for advance warning of sea raiders. They were never baked or dispatched.

Enkomi lies in a plain away from the sea beside the river Pedieos, which was probably navigable. A Middle Bronze settlement on the site was destroyed. *c.* 1550 BC at the same time as Nitovikla and immediately rebuilt. After the expulsion of the Hyksos from Egypt, Enkomi expanded rapidly as a copper-smelting and exporting centre. Mycenaean merchants and craftsmen, using Cyprus as a trading depot, increased its prosperity. They introduced vast quantities of Mycenaean pottery for re-export to the Levant together with the native Cypriot ware. Some of this pottery may have been made in Cyprus by Mycenaean craftsmen. It is distinguished by spirited vase paintings of human and animal groups, more typical of the lively Cypriot imagination than the sober Mycenaean art. Objects in gold, silver, bronze, ivory and alabaster show Greek and Oriental influences. A magnificent silver bowl has a stylized decoration of bulls' heads and flowers inlaid in gold and *niello*. The grave goods of Enkomi stand comparison with the treasures of Mycenae and bear witness to the wealth and culture of its heyday.

Of the greatest interest is the first appearance in Cyprus of a written script. The earliest example is part of a baked clay tablet found at Enkomi and dated *c.* 1500 BC. Because of some resemblances to Cretan Linear A, it has been called Cypro-Minoan. All attempts to decipher it have failed. We do not even know the language it records, though it was probably the pre-Hellenic Eteo-Cypriot.

Enkomi suffered in the upheavals at the end of the thirteenth century. About 1200 BC it was destroyed and immediately rebuilt on a completely new plan by displaced Achaeans and other refugees from the ruined cities on the mainland. They now descended on the island, not as individual traders but as armed bands of refugees seeking a new homeland. But this impressive new city did not last long. It was soon devastated again, probably by the raiding Sea Peoples. It was half-heartedly repaired but after the earthquake of 1075 BC the inhabitants gave up. There was a gradual move to the new settlement at Salamis. Enkomi was finally abandoned *c.* 1050 BC.

The excavations show the city as rebuilt in 1200 BC and reveal the influence of both the Achaean immigrants and the Anatolian refugees who had joined them. The entire city is surrounded by a strong wall built in the *Cyclopean* style of Mycenae of very large unhewn blocks of stone set in two parallel rows; these were topped by mud brick. Along three sides were stone towers. Inside the walls, the town is 400 m. from north to south and 350 m. from east to west. The plan is amazingly regular. The main streets cross at right angles, connecting with the gates in the walls; there is a paved square at the intersection. The streets are laid out on grids; the northern half has seven east–west streets.

The houses usually have courtyards with rooms arranged around three sides. Some have bathrooms with clay bathtubs and cemented floors and lavatories with drainage systems.

The tombs are the usual Bronze Age rock-cut chamber tombs with a short *dromos* and a *stomion* usually sealed by rubble. There are also three small circular tombs built of stone and brick, and seven tombs built of ashlar blocks, one with a rectangular chamber approached by a stepped *dromos*. These exceptions indicate an Oriental influence.

Near the central square are public buildings and sanctuaries built of finely finished ashlar limestone. Ashlar, masonry constructed of hewn stone expertly squared and not a Mycenaean technique, indicates the presence of immigrants from Anatolia or possibly Ugarit. Four important buildings have been excavated; three sanctuaries and one impressive large house.

This last is the unimaginatively named *Building 18*. It covers a whole block in the grid. The front, 40 m. long, is pierced by four wide doors and four windows and faces south. The large ashlar blocks fit together perfectly with no mortar. Around the inner courtyard the rooms are divided by walls of thinner ashlar. Building 18 was built

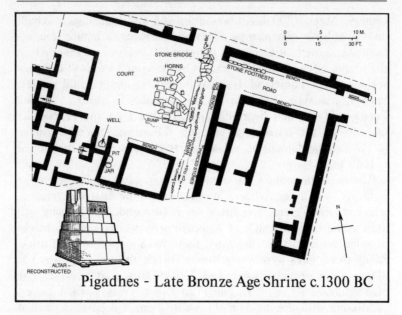

Pigadhes - Late Bronze Age Shrine c.1300 BC

around 1220 BC. Later the windows were filled up with rubble and the rooms used for copper smelting.

The sanctuary of the Horned God has a long hall with two square pillars which supported the roof. Many libation bowls and the skulls of horned animals were found around the altar. On the east side are two inner rooms, in one of which was found the solid bronze statue of a horned god, 54 cm. high. The god is young and athletic, dressed in a short kilt and a skin cap with two horns.

The other two sanctuaries are also built of ashlar. In one was found another bronze cult statue, this time of a horned god standing on an oxhide ingot in a very bellicose attitude, brandishing a spear. The oxhide ingot was the usual form in which copper was exported from Cyprus; it was 72 cm. long, weighed 24 kg. and was a standard (if cumbersome) unit of currency. Copper was so important to Cyprus it was intimately bound up with religion; some shrines have copper-smelting workshops within the sacred precincts.

Myrtou (Pigadhes)

Myrtou (Pigadhes) is a Late Bronze Age shrine not far from Çamlıbel (Myrtou). The road from Kyrenia to Güzelyurt bypasses the small town of Çamlıbel. On the outskirts of Çamlıbel, where the new main road turns

*right at a manned checkpoint, continue straight on down the older road. After
2.6 km. a small paved track on the right leads to a grove of trees containing
the sanctuary.*

The name Pigadhes comes from the wells among the fruit trees to
the south, some of which incorporate stones from the site. In 1947
villagers seeking more material for their wells discovered pottery and
altar stones. The Ashmolean Museum, Oxford, and the University of
Sydney carried out the excavations in 1950–51.

Though today Pigadhes stands isolated, it was once part of a large
settlement dating back to the Middle Bronze era. Around 1400 BC an
existing open-air sanctuary was rebuilt by a Late Bronze culture. In
1300 BC the site was completely levelled. New settlers constructed
the existing Great Court and the ashlar altar. About a hundred years
later, around 1175 BC, the whole complex was destroyed. Though
there are no signs of fire, the destruction seems to have been caused
by man rather than by earthquake. Jars and bowls were smashed,
the blocks of ashlar in the altar were prised apart and scattered,
and the mudbrick walls knocked down to form great banks. This is
the period when the great city of Enkomi was burnt and Bronze Age
culture disintegrated.

The site was unoccupied for 150 years. Then there was a debased
Iron Age revival and signs of renewed occupation from the tenth to
the eighth centuries BC.

Pigadhes is interesting because it illustrates the provincial culture of
Late Bronze Age Cyprus as opposed to the sophisticated, cosmopolitan
life of Enkomi. The first great trading centres such as Lapithos
(cf. Karmi) were on the north coast within sight of the mainland.
They had long declined. Now the trading ships from the Aegean
bypassed northern Cyprus and landed their goods on the southern
coast from Kouklia to Enkomi. By the Late Bronze Age Pigadhes, in
the remote north-west, was a cultural backwater, far from sea routes,
important land routes or copper mines.

Mycenaean pottery does not appear on the site until *c.* 1300 BC
though it had been common in the south-east for a hundred years.
The great sanctuary built in 1300 BC is an altar in an open court in
the old Cypriot tradition. Cyprus has always clung to old customs
and the open-air altar has a long history from Early Bronze Vounous
to the Iron Age. But in 1300 BC an open sanctuary was distinctly
unfashionable. In sophisticated Enkomi the Horned God and his
fellows boasted roofed temples.

Today we can see the remains of the extensive reconstruction of 1300 BC which laid out the great open court with its altar and raised the buildings around the adjoining eastern court.

As we approach the site, the entrance road is on the right to the north of the complex. With good foundations and 2 to 3 m. wide, it was originally walled on both sides. The north wall was unbroken; on the south there were doorways into the east court. The rubble benches down both sides had large, well-worn stones as footrests.

The east block is bordered on the north by the road, the west by the Great Court, and by thick walls on the other two sides. It contained a number of small rooms enclosing a small court. Some store rooms contained *pithoi* plastered into the floor.

THE GREAT COURT

In front of the east wall is a low bench of rubble. Above this are pierced stones for tethering sacrificial animals.

In front of the wall a drain runs northward, lined with stone blocks. Where it runs under the road, it is bridged by large stone blocks. A side branch runs into it from the south side of the altar to carry away libations.

Along the south wall a series of rooms contains a bottleshaped well, 6.5 m. deep.

The altar stands in the Great Court. It was built of finely worked limestone blocks, of which 12 were found in their original positions. About half the rest, including one of the 'Horns', were scattered around the court or built into later walls. The stones are finely worked with a narrow tool on the visible surfaces and around joints, roughly smoothed with a broad tool where they adjoined each other, and left unworked on the back. Using this as a guide, Joan du Plat Taylor, the archeologist who excavated the site, suggested a tentative design for the original altar which was followed by the Cyprus Department of Antiquities when they reconstructed the altar in 1969. Concrete replacements supply the missing stones. The foundation course is a 2.50 m. square and originally stood 5 cm. above the plastered floor. Four upper courses are inset in narrow steps. The horned stone on top was almost certainly one of a pair, the 'Horns of Consecration'. The hollow centre was filled with red clay.

It has since been pointed out, notably by I. Ionas, that this reconstruction is in many ways unsatisfactory. The square plinth and the first course are indisputable, having been found *in situ*. But the present position of many of the stones in the upper three courses does not agree with their dressed edges. Moreover, 11 carefully worked stones, some of irregular shape, have been left out. Ionas suggests that the original structure may have been more complex, involving more than one altar.

The general layout is firmly in the old Cypriot tradition – the cult house with two courts, the benches around the walls, the store rooms, the tethered cattle and an open-air altar.

But the new Mycenaean and Anatolian settlers of the Late Bronze Age left their mark. The masonry used the latest technology; the beautifully worked ashlar blocks stand comparison with Nitovikla and House 18 at Enkomi. The high altar, with its very narrow steps, is unusual. Cypriot altars were low, so that sacrifices could be made on them. High altars were common on the mainland but were provided with flights of steps for sacrifice on top.

Bulls and horns were the cult symbols in Cyprus from the Early Bronze Age. Examples of Horns of Consecration topping altars have been found from Knossos to Hittite Boghazköy. The newcomers grafted the idea on to the native tradition of bull-worship. If the altar was regarded as the 'House of the Bull' it would explain the well-known window symbol barring the lower boxes of the squared motif on the horn.

Set apart in the wide, silent valley, Pigadhes is the most evocative of the early sanctuaries.

CHAPTER TWO

From Homer to Alexander
1050 BC–325 BC

———————— ○◯○ ————————

THE ARCHAIC KINGS

After the traumas of the Late Bronze, a Dark Age fell on the Near East, comparable with the European Dark Age after the end of the Roman Empire. Many of the sacked cities, like Ugarit, never recovered. Civilization retreated, literacy was almost forgotten, and the huts of the peasant farmer replaced the palaces.

Cyprus did better than most. There were successive waves of displaced refugees, mainly from the Aegean. But they came as settlers not conquerors; they appear to have lived relatively amicably side by side with the native Cypriots, each group borrowing from the other's culture until they eventually mingled. The newcomers brought Greek customs and the Arcadian dialect, which spread gradually over most of the island. They brought little of their religion, taking over the strong Cypriot traditions of the Great Goddess of fertility (though the small terracotta statues now had bird faces) and the bull-worship. They adopted the Cypriot syllabary, but adapted it to serve the Greek language. These Aegeans were Achaeans of the Mycenaean culture. So the old Mycenaean language, customs and traditions took root and flourished in Cyprus long after they died out in Greece. By the eighth century BC, when the darkness began to disperse, this archaic Cyprio-Hellenic culture was so firmly rooted that it survived the later invasions.

The sacked cities were abandoned, but new towns soon sprang up nearby – at Salamis, Lapethos and Soloi. These new cities, built so soon after the arrival of Greek settlers, gave rise to the 'foundation legends' which traditionally ascribe the foundation of the new settlements to heroes from the Trojan war – Teucer at Salamis, Agapenor at Palaepaphos. The new towns continued to work metal and to trade on a more modest scale. They even made significant technological advances in metallurgy.

Iron oxide ores were being extracted *c.* 1200 BC. In the twelfth century a few iron objects appear in the tombs; there are many more in the eleventh. Cyprus developed an advanced iron technology, producing hardened and tempered weapons of high quality. There are some grounds for believing that iron-working was introduced to Athens from Cyprus.

Cyprus came out of the Dark Age relatively prosperous, divided into city states ruled by petty kings. The main kingdoms of Northern Cyprus were, from west to east, Marion, Soloi, Lapethos and Salamis. When, around 850 BC, the Phoenicians, that enterprising nation of seafarers and traders, colonized Kition in the south and Cnidos in Kirpaşa (Karpas), they gave an added impetus to economic recovery. The Oriental culture they introduced interacted with the Greek and native Cypriot cultures to produce a unique and exuberant style which was exported throughout the eastern Mediterranean.

Successive foreign conquests did not affect this prosperity. Tribute was paid to the Assyrians (707–650 BC), the Egyptians (570–545 BC) and to the Persians after 545 BC. But the cities continued to flourish and their kings to keep much of their independence, until the imperialist ambition of the Persians caused the islanders to regret their initial enthusiasm for Cyrus.

Site guide to The Tombs of The Kings

The Royal Tombs of Salamis are part of the Archaic necropolis which lies to the west of the earliest city. They are easy to find. Approaching Salamis the level plain is dominated by the Monastery of St Barnabas and, a little further down the road, by the Tumulus which marks the Tombs. Turn right, off the road, for the custodian's office and the small but valuable museum. The open tombs are all marked with numbers.

The tombs were built by the kings of Salamis, descendants of Achaean settlers, during the eighth and seventh centuries. The monumental conception of the graves and the splendid exuberance of the burial gifts testify that the wealth and power of the kings of Salamis did not suffer under Assyrian rule, which involved little more than the payment of a tribute they could well afford. Indeed, they may well have been inspired by a desire to show they could do as well as their overlords in conspicuous Oriental luxury.

The fascination of the tombs lies in the burial customs they reveal. Five hundred years after the fall of the Mycenaean civilization in Greece, the full panoply of the Heroic Age reappears in Cyprus. Such conservatism is remarkable even for the Cypriots.

The best source for the details of Mycenaean funeral rites is Homer's account of the burial of Patroclus. The Trojan War, whether fact or legend, is generally dated *c.* 1250 BC; Homer wrote *c.* 750 BC; most of the Royal Tombs were built *c.* 800–600 BC. Although *The Iliad* was written 500 years after the events it describes, it agrees very well with the details of the archeological picture of the Heroic Age. There is one major discrepancy. Cremation was not practised in Mycenae but Patroclus was burned on a pyre. It could have been due to the difficulties of a state funeral on active service. Both cremation and burial are found at Salamis.

But apart from this there is a striking similarity in the funerary rites of Mycenae and Salamis. In the words of Homer:

Then Achilles ordered his Myrmidons to don their armour and harness their horses; they mounted the cars, both fighting men and drivers, chariots in front, a cloud of footmen behind, thousands, and in the midst was Patroclos . . .

The mourners made a pyre of a hundred feet each way, and upon it they laid the body . . . jars of honey and oil he placed leaning against the bier. Four horses he laid carefully on the pyre, groaning aloud. Nine dogs the prince had, that fed from his table; two of these Achilles took, and cut their throats and laid beside him. The twelve noble young Trojans he slew without mercy. Then he applied the relentless fire to consume all . . .

They did his bidding at once. First they quenched the pyre with wine wherever it had burnt and the ashes were deep; then weeping they gathered the bones of their gentle companion, and laid them covered with fat in a golden urn, which they wrapt up in fine linen and put away safely in the hut. Round the pyre they set up a circle of stone slabs to mark the outside limit, and shovelled earth within.

From Book XXIII of *The Iliad*, translated by
W. H. D. Rouse (Thomas Nelson, 1938)

At Salamis, the tombs have a small burial chamber, approached by a very wide, sloping *dromos* with a cemented floor, down which the funeral cortège was driven. The dead were borne on flat horsedrawn hearses and accompanied by ceremonial chariots, even though the chariot was becoming outdated in warfare. The pyre was raised on a *propylaeum*, a platform in front of the chamber entrance. The flat base of the hearse was detached from the poles and placed on the pyre with the body. All the horses were sacrificed before the pyre and left lying in their harness. The ashes of the dead were collected and stored in a bronze cauldron in the chamber. Amphorae containing liquids were stacked around the walls of the *dromos*. The elaborate bronze harness, the silver-studded swords, the ivory-plated furniture found in the grave goods are all described by Homer. The chamber was sealed and the whole thing filled in with earth. Skeletons of human sacrifices have been found in the top layers of filling. Sometimes the *dromos* was opened up for a second burial.

Nearly all the burial chambers had been looted. Some were dug out by the Romans and used for sarcophagi. But neither the local entrepreneurs or the early expeditions realized the importance of the *dromos*. When the Department of Antiquities started full-scale excavation in 1952, they uncovered an amazing collection of archaic treasures in these entrance passages.

Tomb 2

Tomb 2 is off the right-hand side of the road past the museum. It is one of the smaller tombs with a relatively short *dromos*. The burial chamber was built of ashlar blocks, with a carved cornice of white limestone along the top of the facade. A human skeleton, hands and feet together as if bound, lay near the top of the earth filling. The skeleton of an ass on the floor of the *dromos* in front of the chamber had its bronze headband and blinkers still in position on the skull. Another set of harness was lying nearby. The second skeleton was found huddled in a corner surrounded by small pieces of rock; terrified by the slaughter of its companion, it had broken loose, tried to climb the wall of the *dromos* and been stoned to death from above. The animals had been drawing a hearse consisting of a wooden flat attached to a pole between two wheels. Large jars contained the residue of unidentified liquids. The tomb had been looted, though the thieves overlooked a small silver bowl, probably Phoenician, of the type known to Homer as 'works of the Sidonians'.

Tomb 3

This is the only burial site marked with a tumulus. Grave-robbers, followed by the British Museum in 1896, tunnelled through the mound to the chamber, destroying some of the *dromos* on the way. A through excavation disclosed a *dromos* built of large pink bricks, leading to a rectangular ashlar chamber closed by a flanged slab. Before the entrance is the small stone *propylaeum* or platform used for a cremation pyre. After the ceremony, the tumulus was carefully built up, supported by ten radiating walls of rubble. At the top of the mound is a beehive roof of mud brick which serves no structural purpose, but recalls the massive stone beehive tombs of Mycenae.

In the *dromos* were the remains of a war chariot drawn by two horses, the same type as the Mycenaean chariots shown in fourteenth- and thirteenth-century vase paintings. The body of the chariot was small, with a curved front. It was attached to the horses by two poles, one from the axle and one from the front of the body, joined in a triangle by leather lashings. The wooden wheels had eight spokes. All the wooden parts had rotted, but they had left clear impressions in the soil. Around the chariot were bundles of arrow heads, a circular bronze shield, an iron spear head and an iron sword fastened to the pommel with silver headed rivets, as in Homer's 'silver-studded sword'. Beside the chariot was a hearse, also drawn by two horses, on which the dead warrior was brought to the tomb. All the horses were sacrificed in the *dromos* in their richly decorated harness; bronze headbands, blinkers, breast-plates, bells and side pendants lay in position with their bones. Among a collection of amphorae was one with an inscription in the old Cypriot syllabary which the Achaeans had adapted to the Greek language. The painted symbols read 'of olive oil'.

Tomb 47

A very large, well-built tomb, which clearly shows the typical structure. A wide *dromos* with a cemented floor leads down to the burial chamber. Three masonry steps running the full width of the *dromos* approach a handsome three-sided *propylaeum*. The chamber is built of large ashlar blocks. Looters emptied the chamber and robbed much of the stone, including the masonry along the walls of the *dromos* and the cornice along the top of the facade. A fragment of cornice retrieved from the looters' pits was to have important consequences in Tomb 50.

Tomb 47 saw two burials. The first, just before 700 BC, was celebrated with the dedication of two horses and a hearse. Again the second horse obviously panicked and broke its neck by twisting it around the yoke pole. For the second funeral, about 50 years later, a ditch was dug through the filling to allow two carriages, a *quadriga* (four-horse) and a *biga* (two-horse), to approach the chamber. All six horses were slaughtered at the same time and lie in a confused heap about a metre above the original floor level. Harness of carved ivory and bronze was found with the skeletons.

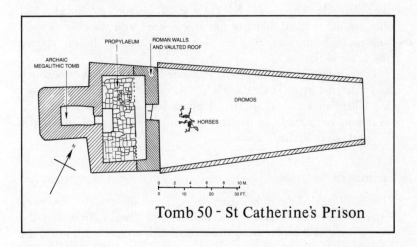

Tomb 50 - St Catherine's Prison

Tomb 50

This is the chapel known since the Middle Ages as the Prison of St Catherine. Until recently it was believed even by scholars like Jeffrey to be a Graeco-Roman tomb. In 1965, the archeologists of the Department of Antiquities realized that the fragment of cornice found in the spoil of Tomb 47 matched the cornice around the *inside* of the chapel. Careful examination revealed clear traces of an earlier Archaic structure.

The building has two rooms: the vaulted chapel leading through to a small inner room, which is actually the seventh-century BC burial chamber. It is made from two enormous monolithic blocks of limestone, carved out to form a rectangular chamber. The vaulted chapel was constructed by the Romans on the wide three-sided *propylaeum*. They built a wall along the fourth side cutting the *propylaeum* off from the *dromos*, and closed it with a vaulted roof. The back wall of the chapel is the original façade of the burial chamber, complete with cornice extending around part of the side walls. The stone pavement of the *propylaeum* is the floor of the chapel. The Roman reconstruction used material robbed from another tomb; the cornice decorating the outside of the new wall is almost certainly from Tomb 47.

When the ground to the east of the chapel was excavated, there was the expected *dromos*, with side walls of ashlar, a cemented floor and the skeletons of two yoked horses, complete with the impression of the yoke-pole. There were few grave goods because the Romans had dug out the original filling of the *dromos* level with the door of their new room. Fortunately they left about 50 cm. and so did not disturb the horse skeletons.

Local legend maintains that a saint called Catherine was imprisoned and martyred here. Since the Middle Ages, the chapel has been used for Christian services, the worshippers happily unaware that their devotions were made on the very spot where the pyre of an Archaic king blazed in barbaric splendour.

Tomb 79

Tomb 79 yielded the richest harvest. Although the chamber had been opened and niches carved in the walls to take Roman sarcophagi, the *dromos* exceeded expectations. It was obviously an important tomb; the chamber, like Tomb 50, was carved out of two monolithic blocks and the facade and *dromos* built of fine ashlar.

Again there were two burials. The first and richest can be dated to the very end of the eighth century BC. A few years later, the grave was reopened, the original chariot and hearse moved to rest against the south wall, and the harness and grave goods piled up in a corner. The light war chariot had been drawn by four horses, whose bones were scattered in the move. The sides of the body were of plaited osiers or possibly of leather. It was divided into two sections, one for the driver and one for the warrior (cf. funeral of Patroclus). The rich decorations of the hearse included five bronze lion heads. Among the grave goods, was a large bronze cauldron on an iron tripod, standing 1.25 m. high, adorned around the rim with eight griffons and four double-headed birdmen. The most remarkable find was a collection of ivory-covered furniture. Two of the three thrones have been reconstructed, although the wood had decayed. One is completely covered in carved ivory plaques; the second with thin sheets of silver decorated with ivory inlaid with blue glass. They recall Homer's 'chair of ivory and silver', belonging to Penelope. A number of large ivory strips, elaborately carved and embellished with gold cloisonné and blue paste, belonged to a wooden bed. Such luxury furniture appears in Assyrian reliefs and is frequently mentioned in archives as royal gifts. A large number of jars and bowls, which had held liquids or food, still contained eggshells and chicken or fish bones. One large amphora held human bones, probably from the first burial.

The second burial also involved a hearse and a war chariot, with bronze accoutrements lavishly decorated with unusual Syrian motifs in repoussé.

All this luxury was only a fraction of what must have been laid in the looted chamber, and gives some idea of the cosmopolitan wealth of the Archaic kings of Salamis around the end of the eighth century BC.

The Cellarka

A few hundred yards south-east of the tombs on a low limestone ridge, is the Cellarka or cemetery of the lower-class Salaminians. Continue down the road past the musuem. The Cellarka is on the left of the road behind a wire fence. It is a unique complex, well worth the extra effort.

These graves are small, rock-cut chamber tombs with short, steep *dromoi*. Because the graveyard was in use for 400 years, from 700 to 300 BC, and the area of hard rock is very limited, families reused the tombs for hundreds of years. Low boundary walls of ashlar mark out their allotted area. Later tombs are squeezed into every available space or carved out of the sides of existing *dromoi*, or even lie underneath. Many small pyres in the *dromoi* contained the burnt remains of offerings to the dead – small plain jars and bowls holding fruit and seeds and jewellery, snakes or pomegranates moulded in clay. Some of the wealthier citizens sacrificed a horse or good-quality pottery; one *dromos* even included the skeleton of a slave. Infants were placed in amphorae or jars and buried near the family tombs. In the fifth century, when Salamis was losing the struggle against the Persians, the burials were small and hasty, with very poor grave goods or none at all.

THE STRUGGLE WITH PERSIA

During most of the Classical period the Persian Empire dominated the Near East. Only the Greeks of the mainland had succeeded in stemming their advance by their victories at Marathon and Plataea. Once freed from the fear of the Persians, the Greek city states led by Athens flowered into the incomparable achievements of the fifth century BC. Cyprus was not so fortunate and remained under the Persians' rule until Alexander destroyed their empire. Despite this harsh subjection, Greek culture spread on the island. The tenuous Hellenic associations of the early Achaean settlers were strengthened by the joint wars against the Persians and by the conscious efforts of rulers like Evagorus I of Salamis (411–374 BC) to bring Cyprus into the Greek world. Kition (Larnaca) was still under the Phoenicians, who prospered as Persian allies and led the pro-Persian city states. Elsewhere, Athenian ideas were admired, Greek gods and heroes worshipped, and mainland fashions adopted in sculpture, pottery and coins. The tenacious Cypriot syllabary was gradually replaced by the Greek alphabet. Cyprus, ambivalent even in Classical times, was politically an Oriental satrapy, but culturally becoming part of the Hellenic world. But though Cypriot kings made offerings at Delphi, the Athenian poet Aeschylus, in his play *The Suppliant Women*, lists alien racial types and puts the Cypriots between the Egyptians and the Indians.

Vouni

At first sight, Vouni might seem rather unrewarding, apart from the beauty of the surroundings and the view from the top of the hill. There are no picturesque ruins, no photogenic columns. The bones of the site, neatly laid bare by the Swedish Expedition of 1928–9, lie austere in the sun. The interest lies partly in the fact that Vouni is an unusually late illustration of what archeology can and cannot do on its own; that is, when it is not supported and expanded by the historian's interpretation of written records. The archaeologist gives us detailed accounts of when and how people lived, but not their names or their histories. Although Vouni belongs quite late in historical times, there are no references to it in any record. So we do not know the name of the palace (Vouni means simply 'top of the hill'), or who built it and lived in it. No anecdotal snippets of sex and violence people the austere pavements. But the story revealed by the archeological jigsaw is fascinating and important. It lays before us an early crisis in the unending struggle to decide whether Cyprus is European or Asiatic, and shows how pragmatic attempts to resolve it could produce something uniquely Cypriot.

The History of Vouni

In 502 BC, the Ionian cities of Asia Minor rebelled against their Persian overlords. The city kingdoms of Cyprus were disenchanted with the increasingly harsh Persian rule and most of them joined the revolt. The Cypriots were heavily defeated by Darius, largely because two of their cities went over to the enemy in the middle of the crucial battle. The Persians besieged and captured the rebel cities; Soloi held out the longest, resisting for four months. (The Cypriots were then forced to join the great fleet assembled by Darius to subdue the Ionians. They are on record as putting up a very half-hearted show.)

Very little is known over the next hundred years. The record in most of the city kingdoms is limited to coins giving names of kings and to archeological relics. Isolated incidents stand out. A Phoenician usurper seized power for a time in Salamis. The Persians and Phoenicians besieged Idalion in 478 BC. In 449 BC Cimon of Athens led a Greek expedition into Cyprus; it had some short-term successes but was in the long run doomed to failure, not least because of the self-destructive intrigues of the Cypriot dynasties. Evagoras (411–374 BC) restored the Greek dynasty in Salamis but over-reached himself trying to establish his authority over the other kingdoms. Against this confused background, Vouni rose and fell.

The palace of Vouni was built around 500 BC on a hill commanding magnificent views of Güzelyurt Bay. The great entrance on the southern (landward) side of the palace opened directly into the central hall of a complex of ceremonial apartments. At the far end of the state rooms, a broad flight of steps led down to an inner courtyard surrounded on the other three sides by the private living rooms and apartments. To the east were the kitchens, with the storerooms on the west.

Around 450 BC extensive alterations changed the orientation of the palace. The northern entrance was walled up. A new road was engineered on the seaward side which led to a new entrance in the north-west corner of the courtyard. This put the living quarters at the front of the house, relegating the state rooms to the rear.

About 380 BC the palace was destroyed by fire, and it was never reoccupied. So much we learn from archeology and so much can be traced today on the site.

This long-accepted story is that the first Oriental palace was built c. 500 BC, immediately after the siege of Soloi, by the pro-Persian rulers of nearby Marion. It was a stronghold designed to keep an eye on disaffected Soloi. During Cimon's expedition in 449 BC he put a Greek protégé in Marion, who remodelled Vouni on Hellenic lines. In 380 BC Soloi went over to the Persians as a protest against Evagoras of Salamis's attempt to extend his rule, and destroyed Vouni.

This scenario fits neatly into the known chronology. It is supported by four facts. (1) The hidden hoard discovered at Vouni was 60 per cent Marion coins; (2) Doxandros, king of Marion after 499 BC, had Phoenician symbols on his coins. He was succeeded by his son Sasmas, a Phoenician name; (3) Cimon took Marion in 451–50 BC; (4) The next two kings had Greek names.

But as F. G. Maier has pointed out, too much of the story is supposition for it to be accepted as historic fact. There is no evidence that Doxandros and Sasmas were Persian puppets, that they built Vouni, that Vouni was meant as stronghold against Soloi (and it seems badly placed to keep an eye on the city), or indeed that Soloi destroyed Vouni, which could as well have suffered from Evagoras when he moved against Marion in 391 BC.

Vouni is a neat illustration of the strengths and weaknesses of archeology. Whatever the true story, it remains a unique witness, the only palace left from a time when the Cypriot kingdoms were torn between Greek and Persian factions.

Site guide to Vouni

Vouni lies on a conical hill facing the sea, 4 km. west of Soloi. At the summit is a temple dedicated to Athena. On the plateau immediately below stood the palace, surrounded by smaller cult shrines. The houses of the town were lower down on the southern slope. The

site was fortified by massive walls running from the top of the hill
to the escarpments.

The Architectural Changes

The original Oriental palace was approached from the south-west (the
side away from the sea), by a ceremonial way leading up from the town
to a wide entrance. The palace was built on the general plan of an
Anatolian *liwan*-house. *Liwan* is an Arabic word for a narrow-fronted
hall often open on one side. In a *liwan* house the large ceremonial
hall is in a massive entrance building at the front of the complex.
This reception room is divided into three sections and flanked by
two smaller *liwan*s. At the back, it opens on a courtyard surrounded
by a columned peristyle. The other rooms open off the courtyard –
the main room to one side and the private apartments opposite. The
arrangement is symmetrical on each side of a central axis.

If we stand at the southern entrance to the main complex at Vouni,
the resemblance to a *liwan* is striking. There in front of us is the great
entrance hall divided into three sections, flanked by its side rooms.
At the far end, a wide flight of seven steps leads to the central
court, surrounded by columns which supported a roofed peristyle.
The private rooms open off the court, the largest on the left side.
The Oriental impression is reinforced by the remarkable bath-houses
in the north-east corner of the court. These were more elaborate
than anything known to the Greeks. They recall Roman baths but
are centuries earlier than the first known examples. The cemented
floors slope towards the drains and there are marks of washbasins.
The first room was supplied with hot water for oiling and washing;
on the south-west wall are traces of wooden benches. The second was
for finishing off with cold water. Later this cold room was partitioned
off and a new room built to provide a steam room. Next to this is a
vaulted furnace, in good condition, with built-in boxes for the fires
which heated the water. The latrines were small boxes of ashlar with
drains; there are two in the cold bath.

Service areas extended on each side of the main building. The
kitchens were on the west and storerooms on the east.

About 450 BC, the palace was remodelled and the main entrance
moved from the south to the north-eastern corner, which brought it
into line with fashionable Hellenic taste.

By two simple changes, the new rulers transformed an Anatolian
liwan into a dwelling approached through a forecourt. They first

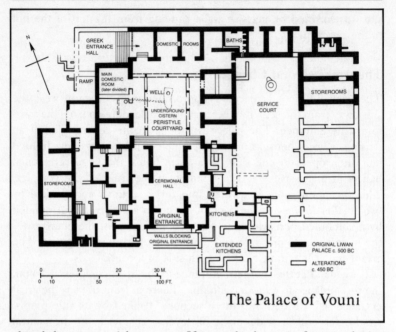

The Palace of Vouni

closed the ceremonial entrance. If we go back to our first standpoint and look down, we can see the foundations of the closing wall. There are actually two walls; the first blocked the entrance and the second, more substantial, created a new facade. A new approach road was engineered on the north side – the present access road. The slope is obviously too steep to allow a new entrance in the middle of the central court, but the new owners were not as concerned about symmetry as were their predecessors. They made a sloping ramp in the north-west corner, leading to a new small entrance hall. From the hall, a wide flight of steps leads into the original corner room of the court and then, up another flight of steps, into the central court itself. The great hall is now approached through a forecourt; it was a neat, economical answer to a cultural problem.

At the same time the range of buildings to the south-east was extended to form a service court, and the adjacent kitchen quarters were enlarged and rearranged.

There were further minor alterations at a later date. Work was still going on when the palace was destroyed around 380 BC. Above the cistern in the central court is a stone stele, intended to hold a new windlass to raise water. It carries the slots for the windlass, but the face of the goddess meant to adorn it is unfinished.

Building Details

The palace is 81 m. long by 60 m. wide. The foundations are stone, sometimes the original bedrock. The upper structure was ashlar or sun-dried brick. The ashlar walls are well finished, but not solid; an inner and outer skin of ashlar has a filling of rubble. The doorways, some double, are rectangular, and the doors turned on pivots. The floors are levelled bedrock with the hollows filled in with cement. In some of the store rooms, there are round holes in the floor to hold pointed amphorae. The roofs were flat or slightly sloping; wooden beams were covered with straw, finished with clay or lime. The columns which supported the roof of the peristyle around the central court and the beams across the open front of the great hall rested on low rectangular stone slabs. Because the floors followed the bedrock, they are on different levels joined by stone steps. The stairs to the upper storey over the store rooms were made of wood. Under them a hidden treasure included coins which helped to date the destruction.

There are no springs or wells. Rain was collected from the sloping roofs through gutters and waste pipes, and stored in cisterns cut out of the rock and lined with cement. The great cistern under the central court was originally a basin type, probably covered by a wooden roof; a subterranean channel ran to a well cistern in one of the side rooms from which water was drawn. It was later changed into a deep bottle cistern served by a wellhead in the courtyard.

CHAPTER THREE

Ptolemaic and Roman Cyprus
325 BC–AD 395

──────── ○ ◯ ○ ────────

In 334 BC, Alexander of Macedon, then 19 years old, crossed the Hellespont and defeated Darius in Cilicia. The Ionian cities welcomed him as a deliverer from the Persian tyranny; Cyprus hastened to join the young conqueror. Cypriot armies helped in his siege of Tyre in 332 BC and in the liberation of Egypt in 331 BC, and were suitably rewarded. Some of the young royals went with him as far as the Punjab. But although the city states were now free of Persia, Alexander made it clear that the island was now part of his empire. After his death it fell to his General Ptolemy, ruler of Egypt.

Alexander did not set out to conquer purely for personal glory. He had a mission to spread the Greek culture he had been taught by Aristotle, about which he, as an educated 'barbarian', felt even more strongly than native Greeks. Although he died so young and his empire was immediately split up among his warring generals, his ideal of universal Hellenization survived. After Alexander, the Levant was permeated by the Greek heritage – not, it is true, the pure Hellenic culture of the Golden Age, but the diffuse Hellenistic. The centre of the Hellenistic world was Alexandria, whose achievements in science and medicine soon outshone Athens. As part of the Ptolemaic Empire until the Roman takeover in AD 56, Cyprus prospered but lost much of her native individuality.

Under the Ptolemies the city kingdoms, which had survived a thousand years of internal squabbling and foreign domination, were dismantled and their ancient dynasties and native aristocracy were replaced by a Ptolemaic bureaucracy. The administrative capital was New Paphos, although Salamis retained its commercial importance. Temples, theatres and gymnasia were built but little survives. The

Hellenistic cities of Cyprus were flattened by earthquakes in AD 76 and 77. The remains disappeared beneath the vast public works of Augustine and Imperial Rome.

Site guide to the Cenotaph of Nicocreon

This fascinating link between the city kings and early Hellenistic Cyprus lies in the necropolis of Salamis, beyond the Cellarka. On the road from Enkomi-Alasia to Gazimağusa (Famagusta) is the modern village of Tuzla (Enkomi). Drive through the village, and just past the church on the left of the road lies the cenotaph. Across a rough field is a square platform with four steps, flanked by a large mound of earth.

Nicocreon was the last, and one of the greatest, of the kings of Salamis. He supported Ptolemy after the death of Alexander and was rewarded with the post of *strategos* (military governor). The following year Nicocreon was accused of plotting with Antigonus; Ptolemy sent two generals to besiege Salamis. When defeat was inevitable, Nicocreon committed suicide. When the news was brought to the palace, his queen and his brothers' wives killed first their unmarried daughters and then themselves. The brothers closed the palace gates, set it on fire and died beneath the ruins. (This story was narrated by Diodorus, who named Nicocles of Paphos as the unfortunate king; it is generally taken to refer to Nicocreon of Salamis.)

A large tumulus on a ridge outside modern Enkomi had long been the target of grave-robbers. Enterprising villagers had tunnelled down to the centre without success, as had Cesnola and the British archeologists in 1896. The Cypriot Department of Antiquities decided to investigate the mound by systematically removing the soil until they reached bedrock. Something had to be there.

The earth was interesting in itself. It had been brought from various sites around the district and included bronze relics from Enkomi-Alasia, old statues from Salamis and amphorae like those used in the infant burials in the Cellarka. The latest finds were dated in the fourth century BC, which meant the tumulus could not have been erected before that. The mound was not a haphazard pile of earth but was carefully constructed on the lines of the Tomb 3 tumulus. The base was a circular platform cut out of the bedrock. The circle of mud brick and rubble was strengthened with walls radiating from the centre. As this had been filled in another series was built above. The excavators left a section untouched to show the method of construction.

When they got down to bedrock, they discovered a platform well off-centre. This is a well-known device to mislead grave robbers and in this case it had worked. The platform is a large rectangle, 17 m. by 11.50 m. and one metre high, built of sun-dried bricks. It is surrounded by four steps, interrupted at one point by a wide ramp. The platform is well-built and is covered with white plaster to give the effect of white marble. In the centre, beneath a mound of burnt rubble, was a low circular wall around a large pyre. The pyre contained a thick layer of ash and charcoal, mixed with the remains of burnt offerings, which included many small bottles of gilded clay and alabaster, golden myrtle wreaths partly melted by the intense heat, spear heads and shield fittings, hundreds of iron nails and offerings of wheat, almonds, raisins and figs.

The unique feature was the remains of life-size clay statues moulded around iron nails on wooden posts, which had been erected in the post holes found at regular intervals around the pyre. There appear to have been 16 statues originally. As the fire blazed up, the posts burnt through and the statues fell and were crushed. Some, however, were hardened by the heat and preserved. We have five human heads and the head of a horse in relatively good condition. The bodies were roughly moulded and hidden beneath draperies. Two mature male heads are recognizable portraits. Two young men and one woman are idealized in the style of late fourth-century Greek sculpture.

The whole set-up indicates an impressive funerary rite. The most intensive excavation has failed to find any trace of a tomb, an interment or a cremation. It must therefore have been a cenotaph – a memorial ceremony for someone of the greatest importance. The finds in the spoil and the style of sculpture date it to the very end of the fourth century BC.

Although there is no written proof, it is hard not to connect the Cenotaph with the tragic end of the last royal family of Salamis in 311 BC. Nicocreon and his family were buried under the ruins of the burnt palace and could not have been given conventional funeral rites. The statues could well have been the dead family – the King and his brothers modelled from existing portraits and the women, young men and children idealized. The grave goods were thrown on to the pyre as there was no burial chamber.

The last king of Salamis was commemorated in the old royal necropolis near his Archaic forebears.

THE CITY OF SALAMIS *c.* 1075 BC–*c.* AD 650

Salamis was the premier city of Cyprus for about 1700 years and has already appeared several times in this story. As what we see today is mainly Roman, it is described in this chapter.

Salamis was founded *c.* 1075 BC by Achaean and Anatolian settlers displaced by the catastrophes which ended the Bronze Age. They were soon joined by the refugees who finally abandoned Enkomi-Alasia in 1050 BC. The usual foundation legend attributes the origin of the city and the royal dynasty to Teucer, exiled son of Telamon of Salamis, and a hero of the Trojan War. A tomb and part of a mud brick city wall from this early Iron Age settlement were found recently to the east of the necropolis.

The next 300 years are obscure, sunk in the Dark Age. In the eighth century Salamis emerged as a wealthy city, able to afford the sumptuous grave goods in the Homeric Tombs of the Kings. It rose to be the greatest of the city kingdoms. Salamis led the cities who joined the Ionian revolt against the Persians, and suffered accordingly when the revolt was crushed in 449 BC.

Things looked up in 411 BC when Evagoras, a young Teucrid, won back the throne of his ancestors. Over 20 years he built up the commerce and the military power of Salamis. He was intensely pro-Greek, importing artists, sculptors and philosophers from Athens. He overreached himself by trying to rule Cilicia as well as all Cyprus and was obliged to submit to Persia in 380 BC.

Salamis was eventually liberated from Persia by Alexander the Great, and welcomed him with enthusiasm. Under the Ptolemies the death of Nicocreon ended the old royal dynasty. Paphos became the administrative capital and the seat of the *strategos*. But Salamis continued to prosper as a commercial entrepot. A new harbour was constructed two miles to the north of the old one and public works, including a Hellenistic gymnasium, embellished the city.

In 58 BC Rome annexed Cyprus, which became part of the province of Antioch. Successive emperors took an interest in the island. Great public works replaced the Hellenistic buildings destroyed in the earthquakes of 15 BC and AD 76. The prestige of Salamis was enhanced by the visit in AD 45 of St Paul and St Barnabas, who was a native of the city. In AD 115 it suffered a temporary setback when thousands of citizens were massacred in the revolt of the Jews. Later, with the triumph of Christianity, it became the seat of the Archbishop of Cyprus.

Most of the city we see today is the Roman city as rebuilt by the Emperor Constantine after the devastating earthquakes in 332 and 342; he renamed it Constantia. The Byzantines added the basilicas and made some modifications in the interests of public morality. (They screened off the public latrines and weeded out the more pagan statues.)

Salamis finally came to a dramatic end in 648–9 when it was the target of the first great Arab raid and never recovered. The remnants of the population abandoned the ruins to the encroaching sand.

Site guide to Salamis

The two early Christian Basilicas on the site are described in detail in the next chapter on Byzantine Church architecture. Page references are given in this chapter, with apologies for the inconvenience. It was necessary in order to avoid tedious repetition.

Salamis is an extensive and confusing site. This description deals first with the most impressive remains, the theatre and the gymnasium. The others follow in a anti-clockwise circular tour. A car is practically essential to cover everything.

The theatre

The theatre is on the left of the main carpark. When it was discovered in 1959 it was completely covered in sand. After excavation the Department of Antiquities rebuilt the lower part for modern performances.

It is one of the largest theatres in the eastern Mediterranean, designed on the same plan as those of Pergamon and Aspendos. Built in the first century AD, it was remodelled by Hadrian in the second century, and in use until the earthquakes of 332 and 342. Roman theatrical performances tended to the lewd and were frowned on by the Christians, so the theatre was not restored. Instead it was used as a quarry for building materials for the rebuilding of the gymnasium. It may have been used on a small scale in the sixth century.

Originally it had 50 tiers of seats, capable of holding 15,000 people. The lower tiers were built on a solid masonry foundation; and were finished with a covering of white limestone which survives on the two bottom rows. Because the theatre was not built against a rising hillside, the upper tiers rested on great arches. These have collapsed but the foundations of the massive rear wall and the radiating spokes

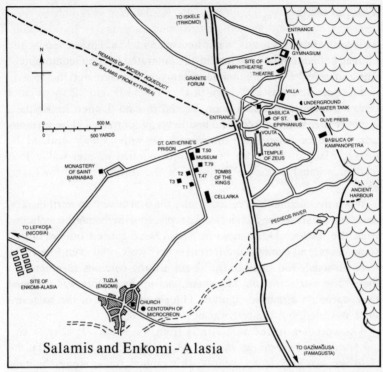

Salamis and Enkomi - Alasia

of solid masonry which reinforced it can be seen behind the theatre. After the fall of Salamis, squatters lived in huts in the shelter of these walls.

Eight flights of steps gave access to the upper levels. The dignitaries sat in the centre seats above the *diazonia* (the break half-way up). Below them at orchestra level was the altar to Dionysius, which has been found in the east stoa.

The orchestra was not used by the players as it was in the Greek theatre; the action took place on the *proscenium*, the long, raised stage. Here it is 27 m. long and only the foundations remain, with the three openings from the *frons scenae*, the high stage buildings which backed it. These would have been adorned with statues in niches, marble plaques and the marble columns which today surround the palaestra.

Between the theatre and the gymnasium lies an unexcavated amphitheatre and stadium, built by the local citizen who paid for the theatre. In Roman times, as today, private sponsorship was encouraged by the state. The oval depression can be clearly traced.

The palaestra

This vast exercise ground was discovered in 1882, examined by the Cyprus Expedition in 1896 and finally excavated by the Department of Antiquities in 1952. The marble columns were re-erected in 1952–5.

The palaestra was laid down in the Hellenistic city; it then had a central circular pool and a floor covered in sand. Under the Romans it was rebuilt with a roofed colonnade on all four sides. The columns were made of drums of white limestone with capitals covered by stucco. Many of them can be seen incorporated in later walls. Two of their original bases can be found at the corners of the far (west) end.

When the complex was restored after the fourth-century earthquakes, the stone pillars of the Romans were replaced with the marble columns from the theatre. Differences in height were evened out by raising some bases, and capitals of different orders were used even when they were obviously too small to fit. These are the columns re-erected in the 1950s, warts and all. The small pool in the middle was replaced by a statue on a marble column. The southern part of the palaestra floor was tiled, but the rest was never finished.

The entrance to the palaestra is from the south. *(It helps to keep our bearings if we remember that the sea is to the east of this site.)* To the right are two very large cisterns with vaulted roofs; stone channels and clay and lead pipes carried the water which served the baths. Through the entrance bear left along the south portico. At the far end is a magnificent set of public latrines with 44 seats arranged in a semicircle. Water flowed through a trough in front of the seats and into the drainage channel below. Stone conduits discharged the effluent into the sea. A fountain stood in front until it was replaced by a screen wall as part of the fifth-century Christian restorations. They also built another set of latrines in a discreet corner behind the north wall. These were enclosed, roofed possibly with a dome, and have a tiled floor.

Continuing around the palaestra, the west portico has ten openings on to a street lined with shops. The benches date from the seventh century. At each end of the west portico are the original limestone bases of the Roman pillars.

The north portico opens on to a series of rooms which were used by the Byzantine builders as dumping grounds for earthquake rubble and unsuitable Aphrodites.

The east portico in front of the main building was the largest and most important. The columns are higher. The floor is covered with *opus sectile*, geometric patterns of marble tiles, in this case taken from the orchestra of the theatre. At each end are annexes with small swimming tanks; one had an inscription commemorating the repair of the roof by the Emperor Trajan in the second century AD. The northern pool is surrounded by a collection of statues taken from the site. The large one in the north-east corner is in its original position.

The main building

The Hellenistic gymnasium was rebuilt by the Romans with bathing facilities, restored in the second century AD after the Jewish insurrection, collapsed in the fourth century earthquakes and was altered into a Christian bath complex by the early Byzantines in the fifth century AD.

In front of the main doorway is a pit which goes down to fourth-century BC Hellenic masonry, the only relic of the earliest structure.

The frigidaria are the octagonal cold plunge pools which flank the central room immediately behind the massive facade. They have niches for statues and for fountains. From the north pool a doorway leads

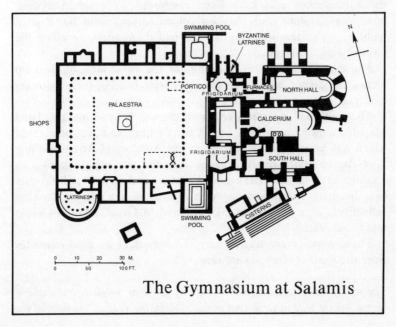

The Gymnasium at Salamis

via a narrow passage with a heated floor covered with *opus sectile*, to:

The sudatorium or sweating room. This rectangular hall has a fine example of a hypocaust – brick pillars under the floor allowing the circulation of hot air. Above the hypocaust a shallow depression filled with water provided the steam. Along the sides are wide raised benches, once covered with marble, on which the customers reclined. Rectangular terracotta air ducts carried the heat from the stokers' room, the *praefurnium*, to the north; some are still in place in the walls.

Behind these preparatory rooms are three large halls. *The calderium*, or hot room, in the centre has not been fully excavated. It is a very large room, 29 m. by 13.70 m. ending in an apse which overlooks the sea. The roof appears to have been barrel-vaulted. The large semicircular basin against the apse could have provided for individual bathers. On the north wall were three niches with mosaics which were blocked off by the early Christians. The surviving mosaic in yellow, red and green has a centre medallion with flowers and acanthus leaves.

On each side of the calderium are two more apsed halls, which may also have been sudatoria. Their walls were weakened in the earthquakes and have been reinforced by great buttresses, incorporating stone and stuccoed column drums from the Roman buildings. The façade facing the sea had three apses, recalling the Cypriot early basilicas.

The north hall has two openings to the calderium, blocked up niches and arches, and a wall mosaic, a wide band of leaves, flowers and fruit.

The south hall is approached from the sea. It has a mosaic, dated AD 300, showing a garland with a female head and part of a scene which has been variously interpreted as Apollo and Artemis killing Niobids, or Hylas being dragged into the water by nymphs. In another arch is the river god Evrotas, with his beard flowing over his bare chest, and one arm resting on a water jar, looking reflectively at a swan. Evrotas is named in Greek letters in white mosaic on black.

These mosaics are fragmentary but important because examples from the third century AD are rare.

The rest of the excavations, which are very far from complete, are scattered over a square mile of scrub and acacia. Follow the road at the back of the

ABOVE An aerial view of the great Bronze Age complex at Enkomi, showing the surprisingly modern grid system laid out by the Achaean settlers who rebuilt the city around 1200 BC. (Sonia Halliday Photographs)

RIGHT The beautiful and evocative site of the palace of Vouni. (Photo: Belinda Brocklehurst)

ABOVE At Aphendrika in Kirpaşa (Karpas) the ruins of three churches are all that
is left of a once great city. St George, built in the early tenth century, was the first
domed Byzantine church in Cyprus. BELOW Ayios Philon. The ruined twelfth-century
church was built over a fifth-century basilica. Alongside are the remains of the original
baptistery, with a fine mosaic floor. (Photo: Geoff Crosthwaite)

ABOVE One of the twelfth-century Byzantine frescoes in Panayia Theotokos, İskele (Trikomo). This is an early representation of the Virgin Mary with extended arms, *Blachernitissa* type.

RIGHT High in the forest stands the charming monastery of Christ Antiphonitis. The graceful moulded arches of the open loggia are considered the finest on the island.

Buffavento castle perches high on the wild crags of the Kyrenia range. Unlike the other castles it was never a royal residence, but instead served as a prison for the Lusignans' political opponents. (Photo: Belinda Brocklehurst)

theatre, past the turning to the main entrance. When the road divides take the right-hand fork.

The road passes on the right a number of fallen columns known as the *Granite Forum*. They are pink granite from Egypt. Then on the left is the basilica of St Epiphanius (page 51). Further on are the remains of the vast *agora*, one of the largest in the empire. One column remains; otherwise little can be seen except the bases of the columned portico.

Near the remaining pillar is a large reservoir, known as the *Vouta*, which was built in the fourth century AD across the end of the agora. This massive masonry structure has three rows of square pillars which recall the reservoirs of Constantinople. The 12 pairs of corbels which project from the walls supported the vaulting of the barrel roof. Water was carried to the reservoirs of Salamis by the 35-mile aqueduct from Kythrea (now Değirmenlik) on the southern slopes of the Kyrenia Mountains. It was then distributed through terracotta pipes.

There is a rough but feasible road past the Vouta and down one long side of the agora. Across the bottom of the agora lie the remains of the Temple of Zeus.

The Temple of Zeus once dominated the agora. Now there is little except a rough mound set back a few yards on the left of the road. A scramble through the bushes reveals the outline of the square plinth. The two bottom steps retain traces of the marble covering. *The track continues down towards the sea and the Campanopetra Basilica* (page 53) *but it is overgrown at some seasons. The alternative is to return to the fork in the road and take the left-hand track.*

On the left of this second track is a smaller *Byzantine cistern* which contains a fragment of Christian painting. It is usually locked. The road eventually winds down to the sea, the *Campanopetra Basilica* (page 53) and the *Ancient Harbour*.

Returning to the crossroads near the granite forum, the road to the right leads back to the theatre or the road straight on leads to the main entrance.

THE CITY OF SOLOI

The Swedish Expedition discovered the theatre at Soloi in 1929 and in 1932 excavated the temples of Isis and Aphrodite, whose statue now decorates wine bottles. In 1965, the Laval University of Quebec

began a series of yearly digs which were interrupted in 1974 by the
Turkish intervention.

Soloi stands on the north-west coast, where the fertile plain meets
the sea, watered by two rivers. Like Salamis, it was the natural site for
a town, and its early history is very similar. It was one of the foundation
legend cities, and was probably founded by waves of Achaeans around
1100 BC. Certainly tombs have yielded pottery of the twelfth-century
BC Mycenaean and eleventh-century BC Iron Ages.

Soloi appears on the seventh-century Assyrian lists of the ten
kingdoms of Cyprus. Around 600 BC Solon is said to have stopped
off in Cyprus on his way back to Athens, to visit his old friend
Philokypros. He gave him advice on fortifying the city and dedicated
a eulogy to him.

This archaic city was destroyed, possibly by the Persians in 499 BC
after Soloi held out against them for five months – cf. Vouni. A
new classical city was built to a new plan, traces of which have
been found beneath the Roman city which has been the focus of
excavation.

Soloi sent ships to help Alexander at the siege of Tyre and helped
him celebrate the victory afterwards. Pasicrates of Soloi and Nicocreon
of Salamis sponsored rival choruses in the customary playwriting
competition. Soloi won. Nicocreon never had much luck (cf. Cenotaph
of Nicocreon).

After the death of Alexander the last king of Soloi lasted longer
under Egyptian rule than the other city kingdom, having had the
foresight to marry Eirene, daughter of Ptolemy and the hetaira Thais.
When Cyprus was annexed by Rome Soloi became valued for its
copper exports. In 12 BC Herod the Great paid 300 talents for half
the product of the mines.

Under the Romans, Soloi was an important provincial city, not as
large as Salamis but embellished by magnificent public works, which
are only beginning to be uncovered. It is reputed to have had the first
public library on the island.

In Byzantine times it began to go down. It could still afford the
Christian basilicas, but the mines began to run out, the port to silt up
and like the rest of the island it suffered badly in the fourth-century
earthquakes.

The Arab raids were the last straw. In the sixteenth century it was
a small agricultural village surrounded by monumental ruins. These
were systematically plundered up to the present century by builders
from neighbouring towns and by boats from the mainland.

Site guide to Soloi

The city covered the hillside from the acropolis on top of the hill to the seaport, now a marshy area covered with bamboo and scrub. It was arranged in parallel terraces, like Prienne and other Hellenic towns on the Asiatic coast, which would support a guess that the Roman city was built on the earlier Hellenistic plan.

In the acropolis on top of the hill are the theatre, the temple complex of Aphrodite and Isis, and a palace. On the terrace half-way down are the basilicas. Below the theatre, west of the basilica, lies the lower town with nymphaeum, agora, porticoed road and commercial and industrial buildings near the port. It must have been an arresting sight from the sea.

The *theatre*, built in the second century AD, has been extensively restored and is sometimes used for performances. It lies on the northern slope of the hill, overlooking the sea. The auditorium, 52 m. across, was cut out of the soft limestone, and could originally hold 3500 people. The orchestra is semicircular in the Roman style and was floored with pebbles covered by cement. Two entrances – the parodoi – flank the platform which is all that is left of the stage building.

The SITE GUIDE to the *basilicas* is on page 53.

The *lower town* has been partially uncovered. The excavations stretch from the modern road to the basilica terrace in a strip crossing the eastern part of the agora. Much remains hidden.

Near the modern road is the *monumental way*, the great road which was the main axis of the city. One of the larger arteries of Eastern Rome, the width averages 13 m. It was paved with rectangular slabs of limestone. The Romans usually set such blocks at a slant to lessen the jolts in solid tyred carts and chariots. Here they are set square. Ruts worn by vehicles show the volume of traffic.

The pavements stand 45 cm. higher than the road and average 4.50 m. wide. They were sheltered by roofed porticoes. The colonades of marble columns, white striped with grey, had elegant Corinthian capitals decorated with spiny acanthus, and an elaborately carved architrave in the same marble. The southern portico was bordered by shops. The doors opening off the pavement are about 1.40 m. wide separated by 2.20 m. of stone wall. These boutiques have not been excavated; one appears to be 2.80 m. by 5.70 m.

The road leads directly into the *agora*. This large public space was paved like the road, with large slabs of limestone carefully laid on a foundation of small stones bound with good mortar. Many of the slabs have been taken by stone-robbers. Although only a 16 m. strip of the agora has been uncovered it seems to have been an enclosed area, with a high retaining wall reaching up to the basilica terrace on the southern side, another retaining wall to the west and high buildings on the east. It was open towards the sea.

On the south is the principal monument so far uncovered, a fine nymphaeum. Only a third has been excavated, but because it was symmetrical, the plan can be reconstructed. It is backed by the massive retaining wall, 1.52 m. thick and even today nearly 6 m. above the agora, which has held back the weight of the upper terrace for 2000 years. The nymphaeum was raised above the agora on a high podium. In front of columned buildings was a large central water basin, partially uncovered. The podium was built out in two wings on each side of this central feature, forming a U shape. Each wing held a smaller basin with a row of lion heads. Water ran over channels in their muzzles and fell into a channel running the width of the nymphaeum at agora level. The reservoir must have been behind the retaining wall. Fragments of elaborate sculptures and Corinthian capitals like those on the colonnades, testify to the richness of the feature, and suggest a possible date of AD 150.

THE FISHPONDS AT LAMBOUSA (LAPETHOS)

The city of Lapethos lay on the coast below present day Lapta. Traces of early Greek and Phoenician settlements take it back to at least the tenth century BC. In the third century BC it was the capital of one of the four districts organized by the Egyptians to replace the ancient city states. It was an important city and port under the Romans and early Byzantines. It was sacked by the Arabs in the seventh century BC, when the population fled to Lapta.

Today it is unapproachable behind military barbed wire. In any case it has been so dug over that little remains to the casual eye but tumbled heaps of overgrown rubble. Fortunately the most interesting relic is still accessible.

Site guide to the Fishponds of Lambousa

Take the west road out of Girne (Kyrenia), and turn down to the sea at the Mare Monte sign. Leave the hotel on your right and walk to the west end of the beach. Below the line of barbed wire lies a low ridge honeycombed

*with recently excavated rock tombs. At the seaward end of the ridge is the
'Fish Tank'.*

The rectangular tank, 27 m. by 14 m., is cut into the solid rock. Inlets,
controlled by sluice gates, provided a constant supply of cool, fresh sea
water. The prevailing currents and winds drove the water into the pool
through the north-western tunnel; stale water was forced out through
the two easterly outlets.

The pool was originally identified by Gunnis as a fish tank, designed
to keep fish alive until needed for the table. It has recently been
suggested that it was a swimming pool, attached to a villa in the city
of Lapethos. Similar swimming pools have been found throughout the
Roman world.

Behind the military barbed wire at the eastern end of the beach is
a fine mosaic, overgrown with scrub.

CHAPTER FOUR

Byzantine Cyprus

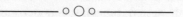

THE BYZANTINE EMPIRE

By the fourth century AD the Roman Empire was in trouble. Internal weaknesses made it increasingly difficult to withstand barbarian pressures. A beleaguered Rome could no longer administer the whole empire, particularly the valuable lands around the Mediterranean.

In AD 330 Constantine the Great dedicated a new capital on the Bosphorus. He embellished Constantinople with suitably magnificent public buildings, provided it with a viable coinage (the gold solidus or besant which became the universal currency of medieval trade), and laid out the great walls which would protect it from the storms to come. In 395 the Roman lands were finally split into two – the Western Empire under Honorius and the Eastern Empire under Arcadius. The West did not last long. In 410 Rome itself was sacked by the Huns; in 476 the Goths replaced the last Western emperor. But the Eastern Empire lasted another 1000 years, until Constantinople was taken by the Ottoman Turks in 1453 and the last Roman emperor died defending the Great Walls.

Constantinople was from the beginning a Christian city. After his vision of a celestial cross at the decisive battle of Milvian Bridge in 312, Constantine became the guardian of the Christian Church, raising it from the status of an obscure, persecuted cult to become the official religion of the empire. He endowed churches in Rome and Constantinople, and was himself baptized on his deathbed in 337. This final commitment had taken 25 years, but since it was generally held that baptism wiped out all previous sins, it was considered prudent to maximize the benefits of a once-in-a-lifetime bonus.

When he opted for Christianity, Constantine gave up the imperial claim to be regarded as a god. But he and his successors made sure they retained the position of God's chosen vice-regent, with apostolic status. Christianity became the spiritual manifestation of the secular power of emperor. Heresy and schism, rife in the early Church, were a threat to the unity of the state, to be rooted out under the authority of the Emperor, who presided at the great Councils. Church and state were one.

All this had a great impact on church architecture.

THE DEVELOPMENT OF THE BYZANTINE CHURCH

Before Constantine, Christian services had been held in upper rooms and in catacombs (cf. Chrysocava page 50). His surprise decision left the Church at a loss architecturally. In Roman eyes, divine and political power had to be made visible by imposing buildings, the bigger the better. The classical temple was irredeemably pagan. A new religious architecture had to be found quickly.

Constantine's architects found their model in the Roman basilica. This was a well-tried plan, which had already been adapted to various kinds of public assembly, including law courts and audience chambers. It was basically a simple rectangular hall, lighted by clerestory windows above pillared aisles running down the long sides. The entrance was at one end; at the other a semicircular projection contained the judge's throne, backed by tiers of raised benches for lesser officials. An altar in front of the throne transformed it into a Christian church. In the fourth century, Christian basilicas sprang up all over the empire. Constantine himself endowed several in Rome and Constantinople.

The original plan was soon elaborated. The centre aisle widened to become the nave. Galleries for worshippers were built above the side aisles and an entrance porch or *narthex* added across the west end. A large *baptistery* outside the main church coped with the rush of converts. The *transept* appeared in the fifth century. This was a secondary hall which crossed the nave at right angles in front of the altar. It provided a large open space for the saintly tombs which were already attracting pilgrims, and had the added advantage of changing the ground plan to the shape of the cross.

It also led indirectly to the development of the Byzantine style in the East and the Gothic in the West. When stone or tiles began to replace the early wooden roofs, there were problems covering the large square space at the intersection between the transepts and the main hall. The western churches adopted the cross vault. The Byzantine churches opted for the dome.

Covering a square space with a round dome presents its own

difficulties. In Persia these had been overcome by cutting off the corners with beams or arches (called *squinches*) which reduced the square to a rough octagon. A better solution now appeared – the dome rested on arches raised above the four sides, with the corners filled in by curved triangles called *pendentives*.

Once the constructional problem had been solved and the dome publicized by Justinian's (527–565) marvellous creation of St Sophia in Constantinople, the basilica was quickly outmoded by the new Byzantine architecture. This was based on the cruciform ground plan and the dome, but there were innumerable variations. The arches of the dome were sometimes supported by eight pillars forming an octagon within the nave. Lesser domes or half-domes sprouted around the main cupola. In the ninth century, the corners of the cross were filled in with lower structures to make a square ground plan, retaining the cross at the higher level. This is the classic cross-in-square. The dome might be raised on a *drum*, which gradually became higher, and was sometimes octagonal. But through all the variations, the Byzantine style remains as instantly recognizable as the Gothic architecture which was simultaneously developing in western Europe.

The divergence between them was not simply due to architectural accident. It reflects a fundamental difference in liturgy and doctrine. In the West the congregation participated fully in the celebration of the Mass and so the western arm of the cross, the nave, became longer to accommodate them. The Orthodox laity were confined to the aisles and galleries and cut off from most of the celebration of the liturgy by the wall of the Iconostasis which separated the chancel from the nave.

The Byzantine church, particularly the domed cross-in-square, was peculiarly adapted to the Eastern view of the church as a microcosm of the universe. The Byzantine religious cosmos was as highly structured as its political and social life. The dome was the perfect symbol for the great bowl of heaven, floored by the sky, the ether which separated it from the earth. High in the dome, Christ Pantokrator surveyed and judged His kingdom of heaven and earth. The Mother of God occupied the conch of the apse, and the evangelists the pendentives. Archangels and apostles had their place in the heavens. The martyrs and saints were lower down, where heaven merged with earth. New Testament scenes from the life of Christ adorned the transepts, and the life of the Virgin the narthex. Small, moveable panels were hung on the iconostasis, each in its appointed place. In the west, painted decoration was limited by the increasing areas of glass, and where it existed was more of a cartoon version of biblical stories for the instruction of the illiterate. In the Orthodox Church, the holy personages who crowded every part of the interior were in some sense actually present with the worshipper.

There are some magnificent examples of painted churches in Cyprus, mostly in the Troodos, but unfortunately only remnants in the north. But an understanding of the underlying idea explains features of Byzantine churches which are unfamiliar to western eyes. It helps to explain the desolate, depressing effect of the many abandoned and derelict Orthodox churches. Stripped of their interior presences, they lose their point. The architecture is designed to surround the congregation in an enclosed spiritual universe and so lacks the soaring, vertical emphasis which can lend nobility to Gothic ruins even in extreme decay.

Because the icons play such an important role in worship the portraits are strictly regulated. Realism takes second place to the inclusion of the official characteristics. St George is always on a white horse, in Cyprus usually with a tiny coffee boy perched behind. To ensure the personage is fully present, both eyes are shown; Judas is the exception. No individual inspiration was allowed. All was depicted according to accepted rules which changed little through the centuries. The effect can seem rigid and lifeless until western eyes accustom themselves to the convention of a spiritual presence evoked through a formalized symbolism. Byzantine art is never pretty or facile.

It is difficult to date Byzantine architecture or painting. While the West was evolving from Romanesque to Perpendicular, the East, though rich in regional variation, did not develop consistently from century to century.

CYPRUS UNDER BYZANTINE RULE AD 395–1191

In 395, Cyprus naturally fell to the Eastern or Byzantine Empire, so called after the small Greek colony obliterated by Constantine's new Rome. Cyprus was ruled from Constantinople for the next 800 years, until the Crusaders overran the island.

Byzantine rule divides into three quite distinct phases:
I) 395–648 Peace and prosperity with a strong Roman tradition. The early Christian basilicas.
II) 648–964 Arab raids and the breakdown of central government. Transitional architecture.

III) 964–1192 Gradual recovery under renewed Byzantine administration. Orthodox Church architecture.

PERIOD I 395–648   THE EARLY CHRISTIAN BASILICAS

To the ordinary citizen, little changed when the Roman Empire split in 395. Roman law and culture continued to be the immutable background to the daily life of the agora, the baths and the forum, or what remained of them after the earthquakes of 332 and 342. Christianity, introduced to Cyprus in 45 by St Paul and St Barnabas, continued to advance against the pagan gods. The Eastern Empire had its own troubles with barbarians and Persians. But Cyprus for once was not in the front line and enjoyed 250 years of relative peace and prosperity.

The Chrysocava

This unique monument goes back to the beginnings of Cypriot Christianity. It lies in a series of quarries one kilometre east of Kyrenia Castle. (The main entrance is barred. Turn left at the road down past the University to the new port. On the left is a UCNC hostel. A path leads past this down into an old quarry, now a market garden with greenhouses.)

This is the first of three extraordinary quarries, dating back at least to Roman times. The limestone was cut out in blocks and dragged down to the old Roman port in the bay between the quarries and the castle.

Before Constantine's Edict of Milan in 313, the Christians of Kyrenia kept a low profile. They used the quarries as a burial place and a refuge. A great limestone arch leads into the second quarry. On the right is a large double cave, with a squared opening and burial niches. All around the quarry are signs of occupation. Holes and slits in the rock sides held beams for the wooden roofs. Rough steps lead down to hearths under the overhangs. Cupboards are cut into the rock. On the facing wall, a double series of niches climbing the cliff once supported a ladder.

A tunnel leads through into the third quarry, which has more signs of dwellings, and proof that these early occupiers were Christian. A simple cross is cut in the face of the rock on the left of the main entrance gate. On the left of the tunnel is a small chapel under a deep overhang. The rough semicircle of the apse is hollowed out of the rock. In front is the altar step and a tomb. This is the chapel of St Mavra. Under the overhang are the remains of early wall paintings.

The quarry chapels continued to be used for centuries after the persecution ended, possibly because they held the tombs of early martyrs. The apse has three layers of plaster, going back to the Romans; the paintings are on the most recent. They have been dated to the tenth century.

Above the altar is the hand of Christ extended in blessing – the earliest remnant of a Christ Pantokrator in Cyprus. A line of black circles on a yellow background separates this from the rock vault showing the Ascension of Christ, lifted by four angels, and watched by the apostles in circular medallions. The writing records the words of an angel explaining to the Apostles what is going on.

A fourth quarry lies over the brow of the hill down by the new port. Again there are signs of habitation all round the vertical walls: post holes, caves with tomb niches, and rock cut chapels. One has several small niches cut out of the rock, decorated with crude festoons of ropework and flowers. This is possibly the oldest church in Cyprus. The small barrel-vaulted chapel is very much later.

The most important remains of the first Byzantine period are the early Christian basilicas.

Guide to The Basilicas at Salamis (Constantia)

Salamis was now called Constantia in honour of Constantine II who rebuilt it in 350 after the great earthquakes. It was the administrative capital, the former home town of St Barnabas and now the seat of the archbishop. Two basilicas have been excavated.

St Epiphanius

The basilica of St Epiphanius was founded by the great bishop at the end of the fourth century. St Epiphanius had difficulty in raising the funds in what was still largely a pagan city, and used the thank offerings from his frequent miraculous cures to pay the builders. When he died in 403, he was buried in the unfinished building by special permission from Arcadius, the first of the Byzantine emperors. His body was sent to Constantinople in the tenth century, but his marble-lined tomb can still be seen at the end of the south aisle.

The basilica measures 58 m. by 42 m. At the west end is a very

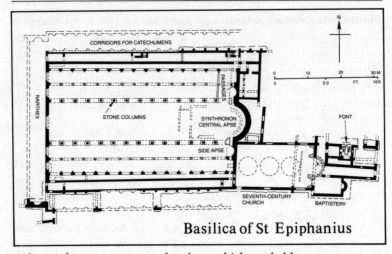

CORRIDORS FOR CATECHUMENS

NARTHEX

STONE COLUMNS

PASSAGES

SYNTHRONON
CENTRAL APSE

SIDE APSE

FONT

SEVENTH-CENTURY
CHURCH

BAPTISTERY

N

0   10   20   30 M.
0   50   FT.   100

Basilica of St Epiphanius

wide *narthex*, or entrance chamber, which probably gave on to an unexcavated atrium. The central nave is divided from the side aisles by 14 stone columns with Corinthian capitals. There are two aisles each side (originally three). Outside these are narrow passages with stairs leading to the galleries. Outside again were corridors for the *catechumens*, the candidates for baptism who were not allowed in the church proper. All early churches made elaborate provision for the hundreds of converts who appeared after Constantine endorsed Christianity. The *baptistery* was usually a separate building outside the church. Here it is to the east of the main building, and is the usual Cypriot type with a sunken font in the shape of a cross. It is heated by a hypocaust – baptism was by total immersion and Roman traditions were still strong enough to insist on adequate plumbing.

The large central apse is flanked by smaller apses built into the thickness of the wall at the end of the side aisles. The apses are pierced by passages which allowed the clergy free access across the east end of the church behind the altar. (This feature, unknown in Constantinople, appears time and again in early Cypriot churches.) This is the first indication of the type of three-apsed basilica which became popular in Cyprus.

The *synthronon*, with benches lining the apse, was added in the sixth century.

The basilica was destroyed during the great Arab attack of 648–9 and replaced by a small church to the east, between the south apse and the baptistery. The tomb of the saint was included in the narthex of the new church.

The Campanopetra Basilica

This church, near the old harbour, is rather later in the fifth century. It was elaborate and sumptuous, reflecting the conversion of the wealthy upper classes. The basilica is part of a very long complex. On the west side were two forecourts with columned porticoes, then the church itself. A third atrium to the east led to a bath building with a splendid *opus sectile* floor in the circular shield pattern and finally to a massive flight of steps to the beach.

The church has three aisles flanked by narrow *catechumena* which connect the east and west atria. Part of the synthronon remains in the apse, and sections of wall containing windows. The capitals of the columns are not Corinthian but Theodosian, a style fashionable in contemporary Constantinople, and supported arches not flat architraves, although the roof was still made of wood.

The nave was floored with *opus sectile*, geometrical patterns made from plaques of coloured stone or marble which had replaced the Roman tradition of mosaics composed of tiny tesserae. The aisles were covered with imported yellow marble. Altogether, a cosmopolitan and up to date building reflecting the wealth and importance of Salamis-Constantia in the fifth century.

The Olive Press

Between the two basilicas is another large Byzantine building with a hall ending in a well-preserved apse and synthronon. The French excavators called it the Olive Press because it descended to use as an oil mill in the Middle Ages. Its original history is obscure. It appears to have had a secular rather than a religious function. As well as the large apsed hall at the east end, there were two storeys of rooms built around a courtyard and a second hall on the upper floor. It contains a number of stone troughs and basins, and a remarkable stone slab with water channels in the shape of a cross leading to a stone basin. Whether it was meant for private or public use, it was a most imposing fifth-century building, an indication that Salamis could still afford impressive works in addition to the two grandiose basilicas.

The Basilicas at Soloi

Christianity was not brought to Soloi by Paul and Barnabas, but by a Roman called Auxibius, whose desire to become a Christian brought

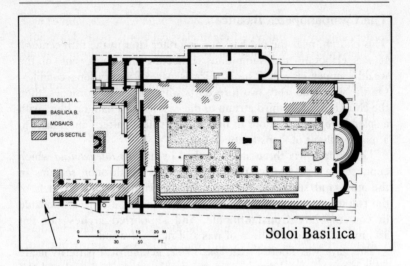

BASILICA A.
BASILICA B.
MOSAICS
OPUS SECTILE

Soloi Basilica

0   5   10   15   20 M.
0   30   50   FT.

him across the sea to Cyprus. At Limniti he was baptized by Mark and
made a bishop. He converted Soloi through a series of miracles.

Soloi basilica is built on a commanding plateau half-way up between
the port and the palace on top of the hill. When it was chosen for the
new state church, earlier buildings were torn down and the plateau
widened by digging away the cliff.

*Two successive basilicas occupied the site. Standing on the rise in front of the
custodian's hut, the two can be distinguished. They both start at the semicircular
apse at the far end. Basilica A includes the exposed central block of mosaics.
Basilica B is much larger, and extends right up to and indeed under your feet.*

Basilica A was built in the second half of the fourth century in the
first flush of Constantinian enthusiasm. It has a narrow central aisle
separated from the four side aisles by 14 stone columns with square
bases. They are irregularly spaced, so must have supported a wooden
roof. In front of the apse is a dedicatory mosaic, perfectly preserved
when found but now vandalized, which asks for the mercy of Christ
for the donors (unnamed). Also behind the altar are three semicircular
brick basins, purpose unknown.

The glory of basilica A lies in its floor mosaics. They were laid
down in three distinct phases from 350 to 500, and illustrate vividly
the progress of post-Roman culture in Cyprus.

CLASSICAL ROMAN GEOMETRICAL DESIGNS *These are mainly in
front of the apse in the trenches which have been dug through the later*

sanctuary; also fragments to the south of the main block of mosaics. These borders employ the full repertoire of classical motifs; plaits, key motifs, swastikas, etc. The workmanship is fine, with small, uniform tesserae. The subtle toning colours unite the various panels to give the effect of a vast carpet. There are no animal or human figures to disturb the severe harmony.

This original mosaic seems to have suffered considerable damage about 50 years later. When it was restored in the fifth century the fashion had changed.

THE INTRODUCTION OF ANIMAL MOTIFS

The main block of mosaics in the central nave. Current taste abandoned the classical tradition including the beautiful elaborate borders. A series of circles, squares and diamonds were drawn out with compasses and ruler, recalling the designs which alleviated the boredom of geometry lessons. The workmanship is still very fine, though the colours are less subtle. Some of the medallions are filled with geometric designs, some with flowers and some introduce birds and dolphins, which were appearing in the East in the second quarter of the fifth century, connected with religious symbolism. The reconstruction was brutal. In the south-west corner of the main panel, half of the width of the original swastika border survived but no attempt was made to restore it. A new border of stripes is simply tacked on.

MARKED DETERIORATION *The southern aisles, under the cliff.* The third phase is dated to the end of the fifth century, just before the razing of basilica A. Here the workmanship deteriorates sharply. The pieces are large and irregular, the colours poor and the designs monotonous and unimaginative. The borders are left white or have coarse stripes. Typically, a red panel is covered with white circles with a blue cross in the centre, joined by small white squares.

The range of styles over the 150 years from 350 to 500 is quite extraordinary. Less than 50 years later the whole lot was covered over and replaced by a new floor of *opus sectile.*

Basilica B   was built, according to internal evidence, between 500 and 550. Basilica A had probably been destroyed by an earthquake: a series of severe shocks in 525–529 caused enormous damage throughout the Levant.

The new church was much more ambitious than the first. It follows the later Cypriot plan of a wide nave, flanked by one aisle each side. At the west end were three great doors, opening directly on to a porticoed atrium; the centre door is the widest. The door sills are single marble plaques. The double doors opened towards the interior; the semicircular grooves made by the bolts can be seen in the north aisle. There is, unusually, no narthex. Around the forecourt was a large complex of side chapels, pilgrim hostels and store rooms, not fully excavated.

On the south side the outside wall of the basilica can be seen to the height of one to two metres, saved from the stone-robbers by a covering of the debris falling down the hill. Every 6.30 m. is a recess, alternatively half-circular or rectangular, like the recesses for statues in the scena of a Roman theatre.

At the east end were three great apses. The perfect semicircle of the central apse still dominates the ruins to the height of 2.50 m. above the mosaic pavement. There is no trace of the altar. The *sanctuary*, the space for the bishop and clergy in front of the central apse, was on a platform 0.70 m. above the mosaics of basilica A. There is a corridor between it and the apse. Two steps led down to the nave.

The floor of basilica B was 0.15 m. above the old-fashioned mosaics, which were covered over and left undisturbed, except where it was necessary to site a new column. The new floor was surfaced in *opus sectile*, most of which has been looted over the centuries, leaving only the imprints of the plaques in the cement.

The quality of this fine *opus sectile* can be appreciated in the porticoes of the atrium outside the west doors. There are considerable remains in the east and south galleries. The varied geometric patterns are separated by bands of marble, much of it recycled from Roman ruins. By the south door the excavators found thousands of golden glass mosaic cubes from a wall mosaic. In the north portico is a stone bench covered with slabs of *marmara*, the local cheap substitute for marble; the end slabs incline to form pillows.

The baptistery has not been uncovered, but there is a large complex east of the apse which remains to be excavated.

Less than a century after it was built the basilica withstood the first Arab raids in 649 and 654. The dates, together with the numbers of dead and enslaved, are given in the first of two stone plaques found in the atrium. A second, incomplete, inscription implies the basilica was badly damaged by fire, but the buildings were repaired and the roofs replaced by 655.

There is little news of Soloi after this. Soloi town was largely abandoned after the seventh century. The last Arab raid was in 912. The church probably stood in ruins until the final collapse in the thirteenth century. In 1222 the Lusignans transferred the bishop with no mention of the basilica. But the tradition of consecrated ground lingered; graves were dug in the debris of the sanctuary and beyond the apse in the thirteenth and fourteenth centuries.

The Basilicas of Kirpaşa (Karpas)

Kirpaşa was heavily populated in Roman and Byzantine times, with at least two large cities, Carpasia and Urania. Two small but interesting basilicas have been excavated.

Ayios Philon is on the coast 3 km. north of Dipkarpaz (Rizokarpaso). Flanked by a ruined twelfth-century church, and seven palm trees, on a lovely stretch of deserted coast, it is the most photogenic of sites.

St Philon, a noted commentator on the scriptures, was in Rome when Pulcheria, the sister of Arcadius and Honorius, became very ill. He was sent to Constantia to persuade Epiphanius to work one of his famous healing miracles. Epiphanius consecrated Philon bishop of Carpasia before leaving for Rome *c.* AD 401.

The three-aisled basilica, built in the fifth century, was part of a large complex including a baptistry and a bishop's palace. The basilica itself lies under the twelfth-century Byzantine church but was twice as long. It included a narthex and a columned forecourt, part of which has fallen into the sea. The columns and capitals are pink marble, not stone as at Ayia Trias. The three apses were linked by traverse passages in the Cypriot tradition. On the south is the baptistry, housed in a separate building. When it was uncovered in the 1930s, the main hall had a very fine marble floor in red, yellow, black and white *opus sectile*, which has since suffered from visitors' desire for souvenirs. To one side of the hall is the typical Cypriot deep font with two flights of steps.

AYIA TRIAS

This basilica was excavated by the Department of Antiquities in 1964–6. Turn right at Yenierenköy (Yialousa) to the village of Sipahi. Drive through the village and continue for about a kilometre. The basilica is on the left in a fenced field, clearly visible from the road.

Ayia Trias is a charming example of the smaller Cypriot basilica. The whole layout can be clearly seen from the low hill at the far end. At the west end there is an atrium or forecourt with columned porticoes, then a narthex or porch leading into the basilica through three doors. The three apses were separated by columns of stone, not marble. There are mosaic floors with elaborate geometric designs, under which was found a coin of Honorius, Arcadius's brother and ruler of the western half of the empire after the division.

The baptistry is a good example of the type common in Cyprus. In Constantinople, the font was placed in the centre of a large hall; in Cyprus, the font, large enough for total immersion, was in an apsed recess against one wall of the baptistry hall. At Ayia Trias, as in St Epiphanius, the baptistry lies to the south-east of the main church. The complex vividly illustrates the elaborate baptismal rites. Adjoining a small hall with four columns is a chapel with apse where the candidates or *catechumen* (who were not allowed into the church before baptism) assembled and prayed. They emerged to be anointed by the bishop, descending a flight of steps into the small deep cross-shaped font, then climbing the opposite flight to enter the vesting rooms to don the white robes which symbolized their new freedom from all their previous sins. The procession entered the basilica by the west doors to attend the Liturgy.

There is no indication that the Cypriot church architects of this period adopted the new domed, cruciform Byzantine churches which spread over the mainland after 550. They appear to have remained faithful to their version of the traditional three-aisled, wooden roofed basilica, right up to the Arab invasions of 648–9, and indeed until the ninth century (see Aphendrika).

Justinianic wall decoration was however represented by two very rare and important mosaics, one in the north of the island and one in the south. Both are of the Virgin and child, both in the conch of a sixth-century basilican apse which survived because it was carefully incorporated into later churches. They are important because very few of the magnificent mosaics of the Justinian era, outside Ravenna, survived the destruction of holy images carried out by the puritan Iconoclastic movement in the eighth century. Cyprus, beleaguered by Arabs, was beyond the control of the Iconoclastic emperors, and the mosaics escaped, in Kiti in the south, and in the north at the Church of Panagia Kanakaria near Boltaşlı (Lythrangomi). Unfortunately for Kanakaria, art thieves have recently succeeded where Arabs and Iconoclasts failed. Some of the panels stolen from the church were discovered in the USA in 1989 and have been recovered by the Greek government in the south. The fragmentary remains of a similar mosaic at Panagia Kyra near Sazlıköy (Livadia) have also suffered.

PERIOD II 648–964   TRANSITIONAL ARCHITECTURE

Arab Raids and the Breakdown of the Classical Tradition

In 630, the Byzantine Empire was in good shape. Heraclius of Carthage had defeated dangerous attacks from the Avars, Slavs, Bulgars and Persians, and established a dynasty which was to last for a hundred years. But down among the insignificant tribes of Arabia, a more serious threat was developing. In 622 Mohammed's flight to Medina marked year 1 of the Islamic era. By his death in 632, all Arabia embraced Islam. Soon afterwards the united tribes burst out of their desert and embarked on an astonishing wave of conquests. Between 634 and 644 they took Syria and Persia; in 642 Egypt; in 643 North Africa and in 711 Spain. Constantinople faced its most dangerous enemy yet, and now Cyprus was in the front line. For nearly 300 years, the Byzantines, struggling for their own existence, abandoned Cyprus to the mercy of the vast fleets of caiques which descended periodically on it shores. The Cypriots, offered the usual choice between conversion and slavery, refused conversion and suffered accordingly. Salamis was destroyed in 649 and Lapithos in 654. Vast quantities of treasure and thousands of slaves were removed. The Arabs never occupied or tried to rule Cyprus. In 688, the Emperor Justinian II signed a treaty with the caliph, under which Cyprus was a neutral buffer, paying tribute both to the Arabs and to Constantinople. For the next 300 years the island was suspended between the two powers. Periods of relative peace and moderate prosperity were interrupted by reprisals for abuses of the treaty of neutrality. In 806 and 912 the Arab fleets made retaliatory raids. There was a movement of the population away from the coasts to new settlements inland. By the tenth century the great classical cities were in ruins and the Roman tradition not even a memory.

During this period there was neither the money nor the manpower to embark on ambitious projects. But while the neutrality held there were periods of relative stability when the Cypriots did what they could to rebuild their shattered economy. By the eighth century they were building modest chapels in the ruins of the great basilicas and even embarking on new churches.

Materials were in short supply. Marble columns were now replaced by piers of masonry. The wooden roofs were renewed where possible but when quality timber was unobtainable, they were replaced by barrel vaults of crude masonry. In spite of isolation from Constantinople, the dome appears in Cyprus for the first time, often perched on the barrel vaults.

A typical example is the little replacement church at St Epiphanius in Salamis. After Salamis was destroyed by the first wave of Saracens, the survivors did not try to reconstruct the great basilica. Out of the ruins, they built a small church with a nave, two aisles and a narthex enclosing the tomb of their saint. The roof was supported by square masonry piers and was originally of wood. In the ninth century this was replaced by a masonry roof with three small domes over the nave and barrel vaults over the aisles. From these homely reconstructions developed a typical Cypriot variation, the basilica with projecting apse, barrel-vaulted roof and domes placed along the length of the nave, as at St Barnabas.

The Churches of Aphendrika

Ten km. north of Dipkarpaz (Rizokarpaso) on an empty shore stand three ruined churches, all that is left of one of the great cities of the Karpas. One, with the remains of a dome, is undoubtedly early Byzantine but the two largest are at first sight difficult to date. Even the great Enlart, writing in 1899, attributed them to a romanesque architect. Today the most probable dating is considered to be the eighth century, and they certainly bear the hallmarks of this transitional period.

PANAYIA CHRYSIOTISSA is the largest, measuring 22 m. by 13 m. Although modest in comparison with the early basilicas, it was built in the traditional style with a nave and two aisles, ending in three apses. The central apse, 7 m. across, had three windows with semicircular heads. The aisles were separated from the nave by masonry piers instead of columns of stone or marble. It had a wooden roof which was later replaced by barrel vaulting carried on semicircular arcades along the side walls.

The wall of the south aisle is held up by the chapel built in the three western bays of the central nave at a very much later date. This is a plain hall with a barrel vault and no windows.

ASOMATOS CHURCH   Nearby Asomatos is a smaller version of the
same plan. It is in a rather better state, preserving the nave and
the south aisle. An arched passage connects the apses, recalling the
same curious feature in the earliest Cypriot basilicas. The narthex is
missing.

ST GEORGE   The small church of St George is of later date,
possibly early tenth century. The masonry is very poor compared
with the dressed stone of the two earlier churches. The west end
has disappeared. The east end is unusual in having only two apses.
Most interesting is the dome, a true dome raised on high arches with
pendentives, which Megaw felt had some claim to be the earliest
surviving dome in Cyprus.

THE CITADEL

*The churches are overlooked by a steep cliff to the south. On the top is
an ancient citadel cut out of the solid rock. Take the lane up the hill
behind Asomatos. Then cut across a field of particularly vicious thistles to
the south-east entrance. This is now barred by a modern drystone wall used
to pen sheep, but is easily negotiated.*

The entire plan of the fortress is laid out, cut deeply into the bare
rock. Gates, passages, flights of steps and rooms with cupboards are
clearly distinguishable. The north wall is on the brink of the precipice
and gives a magnificent view of the shore line.

PERIOD III 964–1191   ORTHODOX ARCHITECTURE

Gradual recovery under renewed Byzantine administration

In 964 the Emperor Nicephorus Phocas regained control of Cyprus,
Cilicia and North Syria. A new capital was established inland at
Lefkoşa and Cyprus enjoyed another 200 years of comparative calm,
broken in 1184 when Isaac Comnenus installed himself as emperor
of the island and made the fatal mistake of annoying Richard I.
    There are no great surviving monuments from this second period
of Byzantine bureaucracy. The official buildings in the new capital
were torn down by the French. The threat of the Seljuk Turks
was countered by castles at Kyrenia and St Hilarion, Buffavento
and Kantara; remnants of these fortifications can be seen within the

later Lusignan improvements. Renewed contact with Constantinople introduced mainland Orthodox architecture, like the cross-in-square and the dome supported by pillars.

The chapels in the castles at Kyrenia and St Hilarion are probably eleventh-century. St George in Kyrenia Castle stood just outside the castle until it was incorporated in the massive Venetian bastion. Four marble columns, with Byzantine capitals, carried the arches supporting the small dome, which has been reconstructed. One of the columns has been lost.

In St Hilarion, the chapel is larger and may once have served a monastery on the site of the castle. It is an excellent example of mainland influence. The large dome covered the whole church. It was supported by eight pillars (two detached and the rest against the walls) which form a rough octagon. (cf. Antiphonitis.) The construction is typically Byzantine. Five courses of tile bricks with wide mortar joints alternate with courses of rubble masonry.

Many of the most interesting churches of this period were associated with monasteries.

The Monastery of St Barnabas

St Barnabas, as an apostle and the founder of the Cypriot Church, is the most revered saint on the island. The Monastery of Apostolos Varnavas which grew up around his tomb was an important place of pilgrimage.

Barnabas, then called Joses, was born at Salamis of Jewish parents who sent him to study in Jerusalem. He was converted by the miracle at the Pool of Bethesda and, according to the Acts, sold all he had and brought the proceeds to the apostles. Renamed Barnabas (Son of Consolation), he joined the Seventy. After the Resurrection he visited Cyprus with Paul and Mark.

Here we turn to legend. He became Bishop of Salamis, went to Italy, and returned to Salamis with his kinsman Mark. They made many converts until their success annoyed the fanatical Jews, who had Barnabas stoned to death by the mob. Mark secretly buried the body in a cave to the west of the city. All knowledge of its location was lost in the subsequent persecution.

In the fifth century the grave was miraculously revealed just in time to save the Cypriot Church from serious trouble. Its independent status had long been a matter of dispute. The Patriarchate of Antioch, founded by St Peter, had Apostolic status and claimed control over

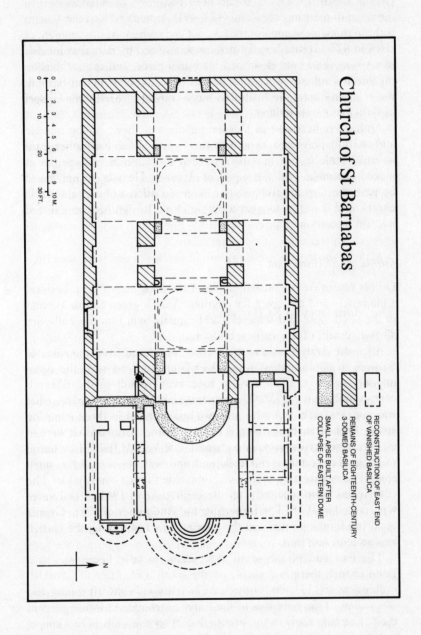

Church of St Barnabas

RECONSTRUCTION OF EAST END
OF VANISHED BASILICA

REMAINS OF EIGHTEENTH-CENTURY
3-DOMED BASILICA

SMALL APSE BUILT AFTER
COLLAPSE OF EASTERN DOME

0 1 2 3 4 5 6 7 8 9 10M
0 10 20 30 FT.

N

Cyprus which it maintained had been converted by missionaries. In the reign of the Emperor Zeno (474–491) Antioch revived the quarrel with a new claim to appoint the Cypriot archbishop. At this moment of crisis in 477, Archbishop Anthemios was visited by Barnabas himself in a vision. The saint described his burial place, and the archbishop organized a solemn procession which found the body in a rock tomb under a carob tree. On his breast was a copy of St Matthew's Gospel in Barnabas's own writing.

Anthemios hastened to Constantinople with news of the miracle and tactfully presented Zeno with the Gospel. Zeno had rather leant towards Antioch, but now realized that the Church of Cyprus was indeed Apostolic and the equal of Antioch. He was so impressed he gave the Cypriot archbishop a large donation to build a suitable church and the right to wear a purple cloak, to sign his name in red ink and to carry a sceptre.

Guide to St Barnabas

On his return from Constantinople, Anthemios built a great basilica, a monastery and a hospice for pilgrims. A dark-green marble column in the south apse and some classical capitals built into the walls, are all that remain of this earliest building.

After the Arab invasions the archbishop moved from the ruins of Salamis to St Barnabas, which had been restored with the usual masonry vaulting. It appears to have been rebuilt in the fifteenth century and again in 1756. The plan was ambitious, if the workmanship was not remarkable. A nave and two aisles ended in three imposing apses. Three transepts crowned by three domes formed what were in essence three cross-in-square chapels side by side, joined by barrel vaulting. The eastern end collapsed and was replaced by a small apse. The two western domes still dominate the flat countryside. The church was again repaired after the earthquake of 1941. A bell tower was erected in 1958. The Department of Antiquities of North Cyprus is tidying up the garden and the pilgrim cells and turning the church into an icon museum.

The east end of the south aisle seems to have been used as a Latin chapel; there is a *piscina* on the south wall. After the Turkish occupation in 1571, the Orthodox Church was in the ascendant and often allowed the remnants of the Latin congregations to use parts of their churches. Early in the twentieth century the walls of this chapel were covered with crude frescoes telling the story of the finding of the tomb. The paintings were done by three brothers, Chariton, Barnabas and Stephanos, monks who lived at St Barnabas for many years. The fresco divides the story into the usual four scenes – the bishop's vision, the finding of the tomb, the meeting with Zeno and the giving of the privileges.

THE CHAPEL OF THE TOMB

About a hundred metres from the church is the grave of the apostle. A small mausoleum was rebuilt in the 1950s over a pagan grave, cut into the rock, typical of many in the area. A modern flight of steps leads down to the ledge which held the body and a central chamber with recesses on four sides and a well. The restored chapel is still guarded by the carob trees which appear in all pictures of the legend.

The Monastery of St Mamas

This celebrated Byzantine shrine is in Güzelyurt (Morphou) next to the small museum. The curators hold the key of the church.

A large dome above pointed arches gives it a rather hybrid appearance; it has indeed been rebuilt several times. Today it is a rare but rather successful example of mixed genres.

St Mamas was very popular in Cyprus: both Latins and Greeks made pilgrimages to his tomb. His icon shows him riding on a lion holding a lamb. He was a hermit who lived in a cave and objected to paying local taxes because he never used amenities such as roads. Soldiers were sent to arrest him to appear before the governor. On the way, a lion leapt out of a thicket and was about to devour a small lamb gambolling on the path. St Mamas calmed the beast, mounted on its back and rode up the steps of the palace. The governor, understandably impressed, remitted Mamas's taxes for life.

An alternative story holds that Mamas was a young shepherd on the mainland who milked lions to make cheese to feed the poor. His martyred body was placed in a sarcophagus which washed up in Cyprus.

Guide to St Mamas

The original monastery was Byzantine. The church was rebuilt in the Gothic style in the fifteenth century when the Orthodox Church enjoyed a short period of acceptability thanks to the influence of Greek princesses on the Lusignan Kings. It was destroyed by fire early in the eighteenth century; the present church was put up *c.* 1743 with the addition of the large dome. The monastic buildings were added in 1779. Surviving pieces of all the earlier phases are built into the fabric, so that it appears older.

From the Byzantine church came two of the five altar columns and the sarcophagus of the saint. From the Gothic period: the north and south doorways, the columns of the nave, two marble columns in the west window and the arched recess above the coffin. The lower marble panels of the iconostasis are the finest Venetian carving, as good as anything on the island. The sixteenth-century woodwork of the iconostasis survived the fire and is equally noteworthy. About the same date are the holy doors on the left and the canopy above the altar. The graffiti on the west door are eighteenth-century; one commemorates the French consul. In 1910 a vaulted narthex was replaced by the present arcade.

Today the church has a spacious asped nave, flanked by aisles roofed with pointed vaults. There are apsidal niches with windows at the ends of the side aisles. The five columns on each side are on low bases and have poor capitals with heavily carved leaves. Two columns under the dome have curious *tête de fleurs* carvings with faces growing out of the foliage. The dome is a half sphere, raised on a drum with six round-headed windows; it covers two bays. Three doorways at the west end are set in pointed arches.

The tomb of the saint is built into the north wall, accessible from inside and out. His coffin is an ancient marble sarcophagus. The space between it and the Flamboyant stonework of the shrine is filled with small icons on wooden panelling.

The area behind the iconostasis is today open even to women and contains, besides the altar, a cupboard full of embroidered vestments.

The Armenian Monastery (Ayios Makarios or Sourp Magar)

Along the forest road running east of Kyrenia, are two long-abandoned monasteries. The mountain road to the airport from Kyrenia crosses the range near Five Fingers Mountain. At the crossroads near the top of the pass a track to the right leads to Buffavento; the road to the left is the forestry road along the mountain spine. It is rough but motorable. After about 8 km. the roofs of the Armenian Monastery can be glimpsed down below on the left. A little further along is a large picnic area (the Alevkaya Forest Station).

The track (one km.) back to the monastery leads down off this clearing. It is very rough but feasible for cars in dry weather.

The site was first used by the Coptic Christians during the Byzantine period but was given to the Armenians in 1425. The monastery was dedicated to St Makarius of Alexandria (309–404). It was fairly wealthy, owning land and a house and gardens near Kefalovryssi, but only housed an abbot and a few monks in cells north of the church. It was exempt from taxation under the Turks.

It was used as a summer resort for refugee children who escaped the Turkish massacres of Armenians in 1895. Later it was abandoned by the monks but was kept as a guest house and a place of annual pilgrimage by the Cypriot Armenians, who gathered for the feast day on the first Sunday in May. After 1974, it seems to have been the target for systematic destruction; every door, window and roof in the cloisters is shattered.

The church was rebuilt in 1814 after an earthquake. The terrace on the south side marks the site of the original building. It is a plain apsed square with no architectural pretensions, though its barrel roof has been strong enough to survive the surrounding ruin. A plaque bears the date and an Armenian inscription. The most interesting feature is the east wall facing the downward track, which still has some fifteenth-century windows with pointed arches and ornamental mouldings.

The Monastery of Christ Antiphonitis

From the picnic site continue on to the tarmac road which crosses the mountains from Değirmanlik (Kythrea) to Esentepe. Follow the good road east for 8 km. until it turns left downhill to Esentepe. On the right an insignificant dirt track leads straight on for another 6 km. to Antiphonitis. At the electricity pylon, two tracks turn off to the left. The first leads down to Esentepe; the second, to the monastery, about 15 minutes' walk. In 1993 the track was not suitable for cars.

Christ Antiphonitis (Christ of the Echo) is unique. The mud monastery buildings have long washed away down the sides of the steep wooded valley and the bushes and trees have run wild. Much of the workmanship is mediocre, and suffering from many years of neglect. Jeffery reported in 1915 that it was in 'the most squalid state of neglect'. But none of this detracts from its undeniable charm. Attempts have been made to save it. After the Turkish conquest of

1574, a Cypriot bought it with his own money to save it being turned into a mosque. In 1906, it was sold to the monastery of Kykko, who repointed the exterior tiles in 1915.

The church follows the same early Byzantine plan as the chapel at St Hilarion and was probably twelfth-century. The square nave is covered by a large dome supported on four detached pillars and four piers on the walls. They are meant to form an octagon, but are so badly placed that the dome is not a true circle, and the pendentives are obviously irregular. The narthex with a barrel-vaulted roof replaced the original in the fourteenth century.

In the fifteenth century, an open loggia was added on the south side. This is of much superior quality, considered by some to be the finest example of its period in Cyprus. The graceful moulded arcade arches are separated by slender octagonal columns. They would originally have been covered by a wooden roof.

The interior was completely painted in the twelfth and fifteenth centuries. The paintings were never of the first quality and Gunnis in 1936 reported they were much 'damaged by damp and obscured by dirt'. They have recently suffered further from the attentions of art-robbers and graffiti artists.

The large Pantokrator and the saints in the dome have survived. The unusual Tree of Jesse and the Last Judgement are almost completely destroyed. The charming Stylites still sit on their columns, thoughtfully fenced in to prevent accidents. Part of the twelfth-century Virgin remains in the apse and there are more remnants on some of the pillars.

Two interesting churches are inaccessible at the time of writing (1992) because of military restriction. They are described briefly in the hope that they will one day be open again.

St Chrysostomos Monastery

This abandoned monastery lies on the hillside below Buffavento Castle. Two churches are linked by an iron grille. The southern one once had a large dome which was destroyed when the church was rebuilt in 1891. The northern church, founded in 1090, is remarkable for being almost entirely built in Byzantine tile brick with the wide mortar joints and courses of rubble we have seen in the chapel at St Hilarion. The workmanship here is finer, particularly in the brick arcading around the central dome. In 1963 frescoes were discovered under the whitewash.

Akhiropietos Monastery

Near the ruins of Lambousa lie three churches. Although access is barred by the military, they can be seen from a distance by taking the road to the right opposite the turning to Alsancak (Karavas).

AKHIROPIETOS   The earliest foundation was sacked by the Arabs. Part of the existing structure dates from the Byzantine rebuilding, a small cruciform church with two domes over the transepts. In the sixteenth century, a major upgrading was planned, but fortunately it only got as far as pulling down the original east end and building the incongruously large seven-sided apse which can be seen from the road.

ST EVLALIOS   Down by the sea stands the Church of St Evlalios, a good example of Byzantine-Gothic, probably built in the sixteenth century. The dome rests on a drum above the single nave. The interior is supposed to be particularly interesting.

ST EVLAMBIOS   This curious monument began as a rock chapel and has been left in an isolated block as the quarry was worked out around it. There are tomb niches in all the walls.

İSKELE (TRIKOMO)

The Church of St James

In the village square at İskele stands one of the smallest and most attractive churches in Cyprus. Like so many Orthodox churches, it is difficult to date, but is no later than the fifteenth century.

It is very simple; a plain rectangular nave with four high pointed arches supporting a high drum pierced by six round-headed windows. The small dome rests on a moulded cornice. Queen Marie of Romania was so taken by this miniature masterpiece that she had a replica erected on the shores of the Black Sea.

Panayia Theotokos

This was the main church of İskele. It was built in the twelfth century as a Byzantine church with one apse and a dome. In the fifteenth century it was badly enlarged by the addition of a vaulted aisle on the north reached through two clumsy arches. In the belfry is a marble plaque from the old iconostasis. The church is now maintained as an icon museum by the Antiquities Department.

It contains excellent frescoes from both the twelfth and the fifteenth centuries. In the south recess are twelfth-century paintings in the Comnenian style depicting the Virgin Mary, the prayer of Joachim and the meeting of Joachim and Anna, with a young girl peering out of a window. In the vault of the north aisle is a fifteenth-century Ascension. In the conch of the apse is a fine Mary, and an elaborate Christ Pantokrator inside the dome, surrounded by angels and flanked by the Virgin Mary and John the Baptist.

THE CHURCHES OF THE KARPAS

Panagia Kanakaria

Kanakaria was chiefly famous for it ancient mosaic (see page 58) but is worth a visit for its architecture. Turn right at Ziyamet (Leonarisso) for the village of Boltaşlı (Lythrangomi). The key is with the muktar *(headman), of the neighbouring village.*

Kanakaria is a very ancient foundation which has been rebuilt several times. Although it is a mixture of periods the general effect is very pleasing.

The main apse was part of an early Christian basilica destroyed by Arabs. It was reconstructed with a nave and two aisles ending in semicircular apses, roofed by barrel vaulting. A dome was added in the eleventh century and in the twelfth, a domed narthex which incorporates an ancient marble column. Some damage was done by unfortunate restorations in 1779 and 1920 and more by art thieves after 1974.

Extensive and sympathetic restorations were carried out by Megaw and Hawkins in the 1960s and 1970s but today the interior is a desolate sight. There are remains of frescoes on the pendentives and in the aisles, but there is no Pantokrator and only blank gaps in the conch of the apse where the famous Virgin was flanked by medallions of the apostles.

CHAPTER FIVE

The Crusader Kings 1192–1489

——————— ○ ◯ ○ ———————

THE LUSIGNAN DYNASTY

In 1191 Richard I of England captured Cyprus while on his way to the Holy Land. He was motivated partly by insults to his betrothed, partly by his awareness of the strategic importance of Cyprus to a Crusader, and partly because he was not seizing land directly from Byzantine allies. Isaac Comnenus, the self-styled Emperor of Cyprus, had declared his independence seven years earlier.

Cyprus was first sold to the Templars then handed over to Guy de Lusignan as compensation for the loss of the Crown of Jerusalem. Guy founded a dynasty which lasted 300 years.

Until 1250 Cyprus suffered from her involvement with the political and military adventures of the Crusaders. After the fall of Acre in 1291, Famagusta became the focus of the profitable eastern trade. During the fourteenth century the Cypriot court dazzled medieval Europe. Not only was it fabulously wealthy, but it enjoyed the prestige which came from its position as the outpost of Christendom against the infidel. It had the purest form of feudalism, based not on the usual haphazard collection of customs, but on the Assizes of Jerusalem, a collection of treatises on the theory and practice of feudal government. Its kings at their best embodied medieval ideas of chivalry. Nobles and merchants hunted and entertained on the most lavish scale.

There was a darker side to all this glamour. There were tales of luxury turning to decadence, of strange oriental customs, and the persistent legends of the Lusignans' fairy ancestress, Melusine, who had turned out to have a serpent's tail and still flew shrieking around the family castles in times of stress.

During the fifteenth century the kingdom declined rapidly. In 1370, the Genoese took control of Famagusta and its wealth. In 1426, the Mamelukes of Egypt inflicted a humiliating defeat and extorted an annual tribute. In 1489 the widowed Queen, Caterina Cornaro, handed the country over to Venice. By 1500 there was no place in the new world for the Lusignans. The ocean-going mercantile powers of Europe were no longer interested in the declining trade of the Levant. Protestantism was eroding the unity of Western Christendom. Chivalry and the Crusades were tales from the past.

Separated not only by race and language, but more seriously by religion, French and Cypriot never fused as did Norman and Anglo-Saxon. When the Lusignans fell, their culture vanished with them. The only thing they left was their architecture which, as might be expected, was lavish and purely Gothic. Fortunately the fourteenth century was the high point both of Lusignan power and of European Gothic. The combination produced some fine buildings, most of which are in North Cyprus.

Whereas Byzantine churches are scattered through the countryside, the Latin are mostly concentrated in Nicosia and Famagusta, and will be described under these headings. The castles and Bellapais are dealt with separately.

THE LUSIGNAN DYNASTY 1192–1489

		Married
1192–94	Guy de Lusignan	- Sibylla of Jerusalem (1180)
1194–1205	Aimery (brother)	- Echive d'Ibelin - Isabel of Jerusalem (1198)
1205–18	Hugh I (son; born 1195)	- Alice de Champagne (1208)
1218–53	Henry I, the Fat (son; born 1217)	- Alice de Montferrat (1229) - Stephania de Lampron (1237) - Plaisance of Antioch (1250)
1253–67	Hugh II	- Isabel d'Ibelin
1267–84	Hugh III (cousin)	- Isabel d'Ibelin
1284–85	John I (son)	
1285–1324	Henry II (brother)	- Constance of Aragon (1317)
1324–59	Hugh IV (nephew)	- Marie d'Ibelin - Alix d'Ibelin

St Hilarion castle, the largest and best preserved of the mountain castles, was the summer palace of the Lusignan court. (Photo: Belinda Brocklehurst)

ABOVE Kyrenia castle reflected in the quiet evening waters of the harbour. The small round tower in the water housed one end of the great chain which was raised to close the harbour to enemy ships. (Photo: Belinda Brocklehurst)

ABOVE RIGHT Bellapais Abbey with its fine Gothic cloister. (Photo: Belinda Brocklehurst)

RIGHT The Büyük Han in Nicosia, built in 1572 soon after the Turkish conquest, is a fine example of an Ottoman caravanserai.

Othello's tower, the entrance to the medieval citadel in Famagusta is traditionally associated with Shakespeare's moor. The Venetian lion is a later addition.

1359–69	Peter I (son)	- Echive de Montfort - Eleanor of Aragon
1369–82	Peter II (son)	- Valentina Visconti
1382–98	James I (uncle)	- Heloise of Brunswick
1398–1432	Janus (son)	- Louise Visconti - Charlotte de Bourbon
1432–58	John II (son)	- Medea of Montferrat - Helena Palaeologina
1458–60	Charlotte (daughter)	- John of Coimbra (1456–1458) - Louis of Savoy (1459–1482)
1460–73	James II (half-brother)	- Caterina Cornaro (1472)
1473–74	James III (son)	
1474–89	Caterina Cornaro born 1454: abdicated 1489: died 1510.	

LUSIGNAN ARMORIAL BEARINGS

At home in Poitou, the Lusignan family carried a simple device of six horizontal blue and white stripes.
Lusignan Family Arms: Barruly argent and azure.

Once crowned, they improved on this by adding a rearing red lion with a golden crown.
Arms of the Lusignan Kings: Barruly argent and azure charged lion rampant gules crowned or.

As titular kings of Jerusalem they claimed the bearings of the Holy City; a white ground charged with a large central cross, the lower arm lengthened, surrounded by four small crosses whose limbs end in trefoils.
Arms of Jerusalem: Argent a cross potent between four crosslets or.

Arms of Cyprus: Argent a lion gules.

Arms of Armenia: Or a lion gules.

The Lusignan shields seen for instance at Kyrenia and Bellapais are based on these armorial bearings quartered in various combinations.

Bellapais

Bellapais Abbey was founded in the early years of Lusignan rule by the second Lusignan ruler, Aimery (1194–1205). As titular king of Jerusalem he felt a responsibility for the Augustinian monks who had been expelled from the Church of the Holy Sepulchre when Jerusalem fell to the Arabs in 1187. In 1206 the abbey adopted the very strict rule of the Premonstratensians, a reformed branch of the Augustinians founded by St Norbet in 1120. The monks were sometimes known as the White Canons, and Bellapais as the Abbée Blanche, because of their white habits. It became the second most important abbey in Cyprus.

It is the most impressive Gothic monument in the Levant. But it must be remembered that it was only one of many Lusignan foundations, some of which were far more magnificent, such as the royal palace in Nicosia plundered and burnt by the Mamelukes, and the great Dominican convent destroyed by the Venetians when they rebuilt the walls of Nicosia. Bellapais, preserved by historical accident, gives us some idea of their glories.

Although the building survived, the deeds and charters have disappeared. In 1246 the abbey acquired a fragment of the True Cross. Hugh III (1267–84) rebuilt part and gave the abbot the right to wear the mitre and to ride out with gilded sword and spurs. Hugh IV was even more attached to Bellapais. He added magnificent royal apartments and lived at the abbey from 1354 to 1358. He is probably responsible for the fine vaulted refectory which bears the arms of Cyprus, Lusignan and Jerusalem. In 1373 the Genoese plundered the abbey treasure. With the breakdown of royal control, the abbots became arrogant. Their perennial quarrels with their metropolitan, the Archbishop of Nicosia, became so notorious the Pope was sometimes forced to intervene.

As the Latin Church decayed the Premonstratensian Rule – once one of the strictest in Europe – became lax. The scandalized Venetian governor reported that the monks of Bellapais habitually took wives (some as many as three) and would admit no novices except their own children, to whom they assigned the monastic revenues. A Grand Council of the Order decided to reform the abbey in 1570, but it was too late. The Turks were already at the gate.

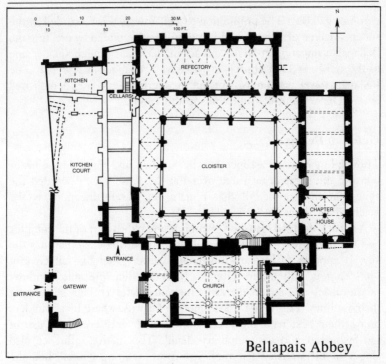

Bellapais Abbey

When the Turks made Cyprus an Ottoman province in 1571, they treated the Greek underclass with their usual tolerance, but destroyed the hated Lusignan regime and the Latin Church with its Crusader associations. Two great burdens were lifted from the Cypriot peasantry: the bonds of western feudalism and the subjection of their Orthodox Church. So, at Bellapais, the degenerate Catholic monks were expelled and the abbey sacked, but the Greek villagers were allowed to use the church for the Orthodox rites.

The church was preserved but the abandoned monastic buildings were plundered for their dressed stone. Travellers in the eighteenth century described the magnificent rooms and cloisters, all steadily eroded. The British administration did their share after 1878. They cemented the floor of the great refectory with a view to using it as a military hospital and are reputed to have used it as a miniature rifle range.

The four cypresses which add so much to photographs of the abbey were planted in the 1940s by the gardener-custodian at the instigation of the government auditor, Jack Cremer. Incidentally, early photographs of Bellapais show a tall campanile built on top of the entrance gateway. The prohibition on bell-towers was rescinded by the sultan's decree of 1856. Local communities responded by erecting the Bellapais campanile in 1870, and adding a similar though smaller one to the newly erected church of Michael Archangel in Kyrenia. The Bellapais tower was impressive but incongruous and was demolished by the Department of Antiquities in the 1960s.

Guide to Bellapais

The triple gateway was once heavily fortified and topped by a tower housing the great drawbridge over the dry fosse which guarded the abbey on the south. All that remains of the fortifications is the machicoulis above the gate.

A small courtyard leads to the church, the oldest part of the complex and the best-preserved. It is usually locked but the custodian has the key. It appears to be early thirteenth century, but like all Cypriot Gothic, it is difficult to date. Early details like the side windows of the aisles are mixed up with the much later corbels supporting their vaulting. This is not uncommon in Cyprus, where local builders doing their best with the alien Gothic made indiscriminate use of old-fashioned and contemporary detail. This native influence also shows in the unusual flat roof. European vaulting embellished the interiors of the Lusignan churches, but the local builders never grasped the importance of protecting the outside with weatherproof pitched roofs. Usually they covered the outside of the vaulting with a coating of poor-quality concrete, made of small stones, volcanic ash and lime, as used on their small domed churches. Or, as in this case, with a flat roof laid out in terraces. (This reluctance to alter roofing techniques produced the extraordinary churches of the Troodos. Forced by the snow of the high mountains to admit the inadequacy of traditional methods, the builders simply encased the entire church, domes and all, with a second steeply pitched roof covered with flat wooden tiles. These protective umbrellas do the job, and provide unusual and pleasing glimpses of concrete Byzantine domes peering out of steep wooden gables.)

A vaulted porch, the width of the west end, leads into the church. The nave has three bays divided from the low aisles by heavy, squat circular columns; the last bay forms a crossing with transepts. Low corbels attached to the columns support the vaulting of the aisles; the main vaulting of the nave springs from the high capitals above. The oldest part of the church is the choir. This is a square-ended chancel with three narrow lancet windows on the east and is influenced by the plan of the mother church at Premontre in France. The east end is now cut off by a poor modern iconostasis. There are traces of frescoes in the Italian style in the porch but no tombs or monuments.

Outside a flight of steps leads to the roof of the cloister and a small treasury, which has three cupboards and a groove for a shelf in the thickness of the wall. There is a belfry designed for four bells.

The monastic buildings were added later and are much grander. The cloisters, which block off the windows of the north aisle of the church, were one of the glories of Bellapais. There are 18 arches, all embellished with elaborate stone carving, most of which has been removed by stone-robbers. The fragments of tracery indicate flowing curves in the Flamboyant Spanish style (Henry II, the predecessor of Hugh IV, and Peter I, his son, both married Aragonese princesses). The cloister is surrounded by the church on the south, the Refectory on the north and to the east by the remains of a large two-storeyed building which housed the Chapter House and Common Room on the ground floor, with the dormitory above. The domestic buildings on the west have disappeared but undoubtedly included a range of kitchens, store rooms and stables with the abbot's house beyond and probably an infirmary.

The finest relic is the great Refectory. The dining hall was the most important domestic building in a medieval monastery. Indeed, it was often, as here, larger than the church. This example, built by Hugh IV when he was lavishing money on his favourite abbey, is magnificent. The entrance, with dog-tooth ornament, is at the north-west corner of the cloister. The hall is 30 m. long, 10 m. wide and 12 m. high, and is covered by a single span of stone-vaulted roof. This is even more remarkable since the hall is poised on the very edge of a precipice. The slender vaulting shafts on the north wall had to be supported by outside buttresses 30 m. high. It was a daring *tour de force*, which has survived extraordinarily well.

The interior follows the plain laid down in the monastic rule. At the west end, a door and a serving cupboard indicate the vanished kitchen quarters. At the east end, a small restored rose window looks down on the raised platform for the abbot's high table. The monks' tables ran down the length of the wall on each side; the stone wall-seats remain. Opposite the entrance is the wall-pulpit from which the reader edified the silent monks during mealtimes with the lives of the saints and martyrs. It is reached by a stair in the thickness of the wall and lighted by a small trefoil window. The pulpit is decorated with flamboyant tracery. Also on the north side are six great windows overlooking the precipice, with fine views to the sea and the Turkish coast. Under each window is a hole to drain off the water when the floor was swilled down after meals.

Outside the main door is the lavabo, incorporating a marble Roman sarcophagus decorated with animal heads and swags of flowers. Six small holes allow the water to run into the lower trough.

Steps outside the west end of the Refectory lead down to a large double crypt with a vaulted roof supported by octagonal columns. It was used as a cellar and storage area servicing the kitchens. At the far end a gate opens on the service road.

The eastern range of buildings is badly ruined but has some points of interest. The Chapter House at the south end was square with a vaulted roof supported by a single central pillar. This marble column and the heavy stone base were uncovered when the debris was cleared from the area. It has a very debased 'Corinthian' capital. Around the walls are the stone seats for the monks. The corbels at the base of the vaulting have curious carvings: Ulysses between two sirens with seductively hanging hair; a woman reading; a man fighting two animals; a woman with a rosary; a monkey and a cat in a tree; and a monk.

Over the whole of this east range was the dormitory. The division into cells can still be traced high on the wall; a window and a wall cupboard for each bed. At the south end is the night stair which gave direct access to the church for night services.

CRUSADER CASTLES

Kyrenia Castle

Medieval Kyrenia had two advantages: the only good harbour on the north coast, and strong defences. Most villages moved inland to escape the raids of Arabs, corsairs, Mamelukes and assorted pirates. Kyrenia felt secure enough in the shadow of its castle to grow around the port. The Lusignans, alien rulers constantly threatened by insurrection and invasion, valued Kyrenia as a supply channel and an escape route to the West. When the hard-headed Venetian merchants took over in 1489, they too appreciated its importance. They abandoned and slighted the three mountain strongholds as anachronisms not worth the expense of garrisoning, but spent much money and effort in strengthening and modernizing Kyrenia Castle.

It is probable that this site had been fortified from early times. Part of the existing structure is Byzantine, though the first historical reference is 1191 at the time of Richard I of England's conquest. The present castle is the result of reconstruction by the Lusignans between 1192 and 1211, and by the Venetians around 1550.

Both castles can still be easily distinguished. The Lusignan fortification was a square courtyard with large square towers at each corner joined by battlemented curtain-walls. Living quarters, stables, granaries, etc. were ranged along the inside of the walls. This type of castle (quite unlike the usual medieval model with a central keep surrounded by concentric walls), was common in north Italy.

The Venetian modification of 1544 was a response to the introduction of artillery, which was devastating the hitherto impregnable feudal castles. The Venetian solution was to enclose the ancient fortresses within immense earthworks faced with stone. These enormous walls transformed the whole castle into a great bastion which could stand up to sixteenth-century artillery fire. Direct assault by scaling ladders was defeated by two great circular towers, placed diagonally opposite each other, where the defenders mounted their heavy cannon to sweep the outside of the walls with flanking fire.

Both versions were state-of-the-art at the time they were built. But while the Lusignan castle withstood assault from trébuchet and scaling tower for 300 years, by the sixteenth century the art of warfare was developing so rapidly that the Venetian defences were out of date in 1571 when the castles of Cyprus were taken by the Turks. However, the imposing additions of the Venetian engineers certainly add to the impressiveness of Kyrenia Castle as well as preserving the medieval fortress inside.

William of Oldenburg visited Kyrenia in 1211 and described it as 'a small town well-fortified which has a castle with walls and towers. Its chief boast is a good harbour'. At that time, there was an inner harbour which separated the castle from the town and provided sheltered anchorage. The Venetian reconstruction turned this into the existing dry moat. The main entrance was north of the harbour, and was protected by a great chain controlled by a windlass. In the 1950s the north entrance was blocked by a long breakwater extending well beyond the castle to the east.

The Lusignans prized Kyrenia as one of their most important strongholds and desirable residences. It was frequently besieged. As early as 1232 it played a decisive part in the struggle by the infant kingdom to maintain its independence from the Holy Roman

Emperor, Frederick II, King of Sicily and feudal overlord of Cyprus. In 1228, Frederick went on Crusade. While in Cyprus he took advantage of the minority of Henry I to displace the regent, John d'Ibelin, and to marry the young king (aged 11) to Alice of Montferrat. When he returned to Italy, he left his Imperial supporters in charge of Cyprus. After a long struggle the loyal barons cornered the Imperial forces in Kyrenia Castle. The defenders, provisioned from the sea, repulsed all assaults for over a year. In 1233 the child queen, Alice, died inside the castle and a truce was declared while her body was carried with due pomp over the pass to Nicosia, where she was buried in St Sophia with great ceremony. The young king could not have deeply mourned a child bride he had rarely seen, who was in any case considered an Imperial puppet. When Frederick sent word that the defenders could expect no more support, the siege ended in the approved medieval fashion. The garrison surrendered the castle and their arms, marched out unharmed, and were provided with ships to convey them and their goods to Frederick's dominions in Tyre. The royal leader, John d'Ibelin, the Old Lord of Beirut, was a genuine example of Christian chivalry, who had even (to his cost) once trusted the word of Frederick. On this occasion he refused to allow his lieutenant, Philip of Novare, a brilliant young knight with literary pretensions, to compose one of his famous satiric verses at the expense of the defeated.

In 1349, Hugh IV, a pious but vindictive monarch, had trouble with his young son Peter, who was to become the most glamorous of the crusading Lusignans. With his young brother John, Peter ran away to Europe pursued by two royal galleys. They got as far as Rome before they were caught and brought back. They were thrown into the dungeons of Kyrenia but released after the Pope intervened. They were lucky: their tutor lost a hand and a foot and was hanged.

Many distinguished prisoners disappeared in the dungeons of Kyrenia. Medieval sensibilities disliked public executions. They much preferred a hired assassin or a quiet oubliette where political opponents could be discreetly starved. Henry II had a bitter struggle with his brother Amaury. In 1310, Amaury was murdered. All his supporters were shut up in Kyrenia by an implacable Henry, with the words, 'As you have behaved to us we shall behave to you.' They all starved to death in the dungeons. A chronicler records that slaves carried the rotting bodies on a carpet to a nearby church for burial. The oubliettes of Kyrenia can be seen immediately beneath the windows of the palace apartments. The imprisonment of Aumery de Mimars in 1343 had a happier result. He employed his enforced leisure in transcribing the only surviving copy of the *Gestes des Chiprois*.

From 1233 to 1374 the kingdom flourished and the walls of Kyrenia were at peace. Acre, the last bastion of Christendom in the Levant, fell in 1291. For at least a hundred years the ladies of Cyprus wore long black hooded cloaks in mourning for Frankish Syria. But in fact a burden had been lifted from Cyprus. There were no more expensive adventures to the mainland. Famagusta became the entrepôt for the East; merchants and nobility made huge fortunes.

The royal apartments in the castle lifted their pointed roofs over the west wall, the Gothic windows looked down on the prosperous port. There was the usual backdrop of medieval disasters: vicious quarrels in the royal family; drought, famine and blight; and a terrible outbreak of the Black Death in 1349. But these years, culminating in the brilliant reign of Peter I, were the apogee of the Lusignan era.

Peter was charismatic, clever and physically attractive and won the admiration of Europe for his Crusading exploits. But he was always obsessive and unstable, and on his return to Cyprus became brutally and dangerously paranoid. In 1369 he was murdered by his barons with the knowledge of his brothers. The rot set in and Kyrenia again saw turbulent action. In 1374, the Republic of Genoa sent a large army. It quickly captured the boy king, Peter II, overran the country and pillaged Nicosia. His uncle, James, held out in Kyrenia. At first, the Genoese were supported by the queen mother, Eleanor of Aragon, who hoped to use them to avenge the murder of her husband, Peter I. She changed sides when their success threatened her son's crown. Eleanor was a devious, violent and vindictive woman but she was brave and resourceful. She offered to help the Genoese take Kyrenia and rode at the head of their troops from Nicosia, mounted on the late king's mule Margarita, the fastest in Cyprus. At the top of the pass, she signed to her squire to fix her spurs, threw her leg over astride, and pelted down the hill, her wide skirts billowing, into the castle.

James and the queen held out for four months against the most determined attacks ever launched against the castle. In February, the Genoese herald announced a reward of 1000 besants for the first attacker to set the king's banner on the walls, 500 for the second and so on. As each prize was called the defenders produced a banner and claimed the reward. This by-play was followed by an assault in force which was repulsed after two and a half hours. That night 15 volunteers sallied out of the castle and set fire to the brushwood filling up the fosse at the base of the walls.

Genoese ships carrying mangonels hurled heavy stones to batter the masonry. The defenders let down the drawbridge, first equipping it with an ingenious device involving a pivot and counterpoise, which hurled attackers into the ditch.

In March there was a big attack by land and sea. A galley broke through the harbour chain but was repulsed. The Genoese brought up four enormous fighting towers – the *Sow*, which hurled stones; the *Cat*, which had three storeys and a battering ram; the *Falcon*, with protected scaling ladders; and the *Cage*, which carried crossbowmen so high they could fire over the walls. The Bulgarian mercenaries, unkempt but fearless, made a sortie from the castle, burned the *Falcon* and the *Cage* and overturned the *Sow*. That night the defenders collected the nails from the ruined machines, put them point up in the planks and buried them in sand in the fosse – an early anti-personnel device. The Genoese built a platform between the masts of two ships to shoot over the walls but a lucky trébuchet shot sent it into the sea.

Boring days were enlivened by the exchange of insults, offers to settle by open combat, and the entertainment of envoys, who were lavishly feasted for six days to prove the defenders were not short of food (they were). Eventually the Genoese gave up and retired to Nicosia.

Unfortunately, the Genoese still held the young king, who was forced to make a settlement. The queen mother joined her son in Nicosia and James was ordered to surrender Kyrenia. He was given a safe conduct to Europe. But the days of the high chivalry of the Lord of Beirut were over: the Genoese broke their oath, captured James and imprisoned him in Genoa.

In 1426, the Mamelukes of Egypt invaded Cyprus. They defeated and captured King Janus and pillaged Nicosia. The archbishop, a younger brother who acted as regent, took refuge in Kyrenia with the royal family and the crown jewels. The Mamelukes got as far as the pass but decided the castle was too strong and sailed for Egypt with 6000 slaves including the king.

In 1460, the young Queen Charlotte was besieged in Kyrenia Castle for three years by her half-brother James the Bastard, who had usurped the crown. The walls of Kyrenia served her well and she kept hold of this last piece of her kingdom until starvation and treachery forced its surrender during one of her absences in Europe to raise support.

In 1554, the new Venetian rulers strengthened the castle but it made

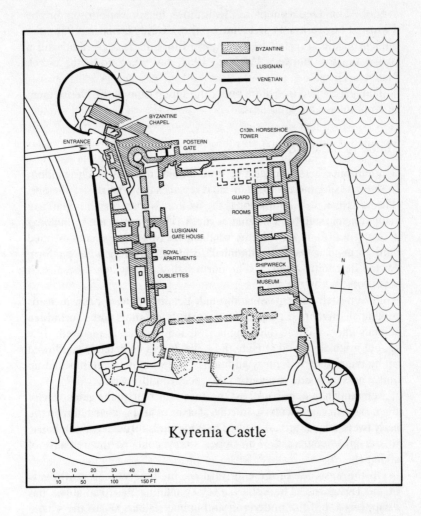

BYZANTINE

LUSIGNAN

VENETIAN

BYZANTINE
CHAPEL

C13th. HORSESHOE
TOWER

ENTRANCE

POSTERN
GATE

GUARD

ROOMS

LUSIGNAN
GATE HOUSE

ROYAL
APARTMENTS

SHIPWRECK

OUBLIETTES

MUSEUM

N

Kyrenia Castle

0   10   20   30   40   50 M
10   50   100   150 FT

little attempt to resist the Turkish invasion in 1570. The Turkish admiral who received the surrender lies in a tomb within the entrance of the castle.

The Turkish forces used the castle as a prison and a barracks, retiring within it at night. In 1765, the commandant revolted and it was again under assault but surrendered after a siege.

In 1878, the British leased the island from the Porte. At first a barracks and prison, the castle later became a police barracks and

school. The Department of Antiquities began restoration in the
1950s. The work was held up by the EOKA crisis in 1955; the
ancient castle reverted to its historic function as a garrison and a
political prison. Between 1963 and 1967, part was used by the Greek
National Guard.

Today it is open to visitors under the supervision of the Department
of Antiquities and Museums.

Guide to the Castle

The entrance is on the west or town side of the castle. The modern
bridge crossing the dry fosse or moat replaces the original drawbridge.
The massive wall confronting the visitor is part of the Venetian
ramparts encasing the Lusignan fortress. They were made by building
a strong wall 6 m. outside the original; the space between was filled
with earth to withstand cannonballs and to provide a wide platform
for the defending artillery. The north wall was not altered because it
was protected by the sea.

Turning left after passing through the first gate, a passage leads
to a small Byzantine chapel. Three marble columns with Corinthian
capitals carry arches which support a dome, recently restored. The
chapel originally stood outside the walls. It was completely swallowed
up by the sixteenth-century additions. The windows were blocked up
and a passage made through to the great round tower.

Retracing our steps back past the entry we come to the gatehouse of
the Lusignan castle with two medieval coats of arms, moved here in the
early twentieth century. A vaulted passage leads through the gatehouse
to the great courtyard. The upper storey contains the remains of
a chapel.

On the west side of the courtyard are the long vaulted apartments
of the Lusignans. The upper storey containing the royal suites has
disappeared, but the undercroft and oubliettes survive. In the south-
west corner is a Byzantine tower and a passage leading to the great
Venetian bastion, the central strongpoint of the artillery fortress. The
south ward had been filled up with earth; it was excavated in 1952–3.
The postern leading to the main court is ornamented with carved
lions, probably Roman. The horseshoe-shaped tower in the southern
part of the court is Byzantine.

Along the east side are the medieval guardrooms. They have been
well restored and now house the unique Ship Museum (p. 85) opened
in 1976 by the Turkish Federated State of Kıbrıs.

Beyond, in the north-east corner, is one of the original corner towers of the Lusignan fortress. The Venetians did not think artillery attack would ever come from the sea and left this corner and the north curtain-wall in their medieval form. The tower is a horseshoe, set at an angle, with two vaulted halls above dungeons. The rooms are lighted by deeply splayed arrow slits, similar to those at Kantara. The upper hall opens on to the sea wall. The battlements along this curtain-wall are in the form of hollow boxes to protect bowmen firing through the slits. The west end of the wall once commanded the harbour and the town. It now leads us back to the gatehouse and the Venetian fortifications.

On the east side of the castle is the Ship Museum, which houses a trading galley from about 300 BC – the time of Alexander the Great – the oldest ever recovered. It was found by a local diver about half a mile off Kyrenia. The University of Pennsylvania raised the hull, complete with cargo, in 1969. The pine timbers have been carefully preserved, reassembled and exhibited in an air-conditioned hall. In another room is a modern replica of the middle section, showing the method of construction: the planking was built up first, then held in place by the ribs secured with copper spikes. Also exhibited are some of the cargo of 400 amphorae of wine, 9000 well-preserved almonds, the ballast of 29 millstones and the eating implements of the crew of four. There was no sign of bodies, so presumably the seamen swam to safety when the galley sank.

The Castle of St Hilarion

The Lusignans maintained three castles along the limestone ridge of the Kyrenia mountains. The largest, best-maintained and most accessible is St Hilarion. It is named not after St Hilarion the Great, the well-documented founder of eastern monasticism, but after an obscure hermit of the same name, who was expelled from Palestine by the Arab invasion and sought sanctuary in Cyprus. His faithful disciple discovered a suitably remote retreat in the 'lofty and precipitous mountains of the northern range' (Hackett) and here the holy man passed his final years. On his death an Orthodox monastery was built around his tomb to accommodate his relics and to provide shelter for pilgrims. The Byzantines made the monastery into a castle, probably in the eleventh century, at the same time as they fortified Kyrenia, Kantara and Buffavento. It was handed over to Richard I of England by Isaac Comnenus in 1191.

The road to Hilarion is signposted on the right of the main road from Girne
(Kyrenia) to Lefkoşa (Nicosia) about 3 miles (5 km.) from Girne at the top
of the pass.

The castle in its present form was built in 1228 by John d'Ibelin,
the Old Lord of Beirut, Regent to the Kingdom of Cyprus. It was
intended to be a strong retreat where the young King Henry I and
his family could hold out against the supporters of Frederick II. It
changed hands several times during the struggle. In 1230, when it
was held by the Imperialists, the loyalist knight, Philip de Novare
was wounded by an arrow and lay out all night on the rocks facing
the castle. He passed the time composing and signing satires and
insulting verses to annoy the garrison. Frederick's army was defeated
in 1232 at Aghirda in the pass, forced to retreat to Kyrenia and finally
capitulated in 1233.

During the long period of peace and prosperity from 1233 to 1373,
Hilarion became Dieu d'Amour (Cupid's Castle), the summer palace
of the Lusignan court.

Two cultures made up medieval Cyprus. The indigenous population,
reduced to serfdom, spoke mainly Greek and clung obstinately to
their exiled Orthodox bishops. They are ignored by the chroniclers;
it is easy to forget that they were always there, hanging stubbornly
on in their miserable hovels, to reappear when the Latins were only
a memory. The Latin nobility were Roman Catholic, spoke French
or Italian, and were organized into a classic version of the West
European feudal system, as laid down in the Assizes of Jerusalem.
Some were knights and burgesses, who had lost lands and possessions
in the Muslim advance and were given fiefs to encourage them to
settle in the new kingdom. Then there were the great Crusader
princes of Outremer, who, as the Turks conquered their Levantine
fiefs of Antioch, Tyre, Sidon and Beirut, retired to their Cypriot
estates. They brought with them their empty titles and the oriental
habits they had learnt from their contact with the highly cultured
Abbasid civilization. John II's wife, Queen Helena Palaeologina, a
Byzantine princess of impeccable lineage, swore fluently in French,
Arabic and Greek (she also bit off the nose of her husband's mistress,
Mary of Patras).

It was a bizarre mixture and never began to coalesce into a nation
such as Normans and Saxons were forging in England. But for a
couple of centuries it flowered into the most extravagant, cultured
and decadent court in Europe. It fascinated and repelled the rest

of Europe, and achieved a renown far greater than its size and power deserved. Today, perhaps the best place to recall that past splendour is the belvedere of St Hilarion on a summer's day. The court passed the hot afternoons looking at the incomparable view, playing chess, strumming lutes and listening to poetry. The barons indulged their passion for the chase, riding out with their hawks on their wrists to camp in the hills for weeks at a time. They took with them their hunting leopards to run down the mouflon (wild sheep) and their pampered hounds, each couple in the care of its own servant. Down below the emblazoned pennants hung limply over the silken pavilions of the tourney ground and the supply trains of mules and camels plodded past. And in the background rose from the vast outer bailey the constant murmur from the knights, squires, cooks, scullions, merchants, soldiers, grooms, slaves, scholars and musicians who serviced the most exotic court in Europe.

Hilarion was also of course a military stronghold. Though not the ideal site for a castle, it had considerable strategic value. To stop on the road from Kyrenia to Nicosia, at the spot where the road to St Hilarion branches off on the right, is to appreciate how a force based on the castle could dominate the pass through the mountains. During the Genoese invasion of 1373, while the young king was held prisoner, the queen mother and his uncle James held out in Kyrenia and his other uncle, John, Prince of Antioch, held Hilarion with his faithful Bulgarian mercenaries. They made many successful sorties against the supply trains coming from Nicosia to the Genoese besieging Kyrenia. On 24 February 1374 they captured 20 scaling ladders and on the 28th a large camel convoy. When the besiegers eventually gave up and retired to Nicosia, they were severely mauled in the pass by the Bulgarians.

Eleanor of Aragon, the queen mother, was still nursing her hopes of vengeance on the murderers of her husband, Peter I, and had already persuaded the Genoese to behead the barons who had stabbed him to death. She believed his brothers, James and John of Antioch, were also involved. She was prepared to cooperate with them during the Genoese war, but she had not forgotten. After the treaty of 1374 and the surrender of Kyrenia, James was imprisoned in Genoa. She turned her attention to John, still ensconced in Hilarion. She had been so afraid that he and his Bulgarians would seize her on her way to Nicosia through the pass after the siege of Kyrenia, that she sent for him to take a mutual oath of peace at a special mass. Back in Nicosia, she persuaded James that his Bulgarians were plotting to murder him.

According to the chroniclers, he had them thrown down a precipice
from what is today known as Prince John's Tower. Defenestration
was an accepted punishment for treachery. But it seems unlikely that
a large body of tough and seasoned fighters would meekly line up to
be dealt with one by one. Sir George Hill considered it more probable
that the officers went through the window and the rank and file were
disbanded. Either way, John of Antioch lost his best weapon.

His next move was so naive that some historians consider him
insane, although he had been a popular regent and an excellent
soldier. On the queen's invitation he left St Hilarion for Nicosia.
Perhaps he believed the oaths they had taken on the Body of Christ
that they were now at peace. Against the advice of all his friends he
accepted an invitation to dine with the queen and the young king.
They ate in the room where Peter I had been killed. As the meal
ended Eleanor uncovered a dish containing the blood-stained shirt
of her husband, with the words, 'Sir Prince, do you know whose
is this shirt?' This was the signal for the concealed knights to leap
out and stab John to death. Eleanor was not a woman to forget a
grievance.

After Peter II married in 1378, Eleanor quarrelled with his wealthy
wife, Valentina, and was sent back to Aragon, where she lived until
1417.

When the Venetians occupied the island, the active life of
St Hilarion came to an end. They dismantled the castle to save the
cost of a garrison and to prevent it being used by Turkish invaders
from the mainland.

Guide to St Hilarion

The castle was designed by the Byzantines to enclose the entire
summit of the mountain, known as Didymas because of the twin
peaks. There are three distinct sections.

The outer wall stretches for about a quarter of a mile with seven
semicircular towers. It is original Byzantine work roughly built with
rubble masonry. It encloses a very large bailey, covering the southern
slope. Here were the barracks and stables, and judging by the traces
of walls and huts, a small village of dependants. The defences of this
first section are not impressive. The rubble walls were not capable
of withstanding a sophisticated attack and there was of course no
moat or fosse. Today the outgate with a restored gatehouse leads
into a very small barbican protecting the main entrance, which is

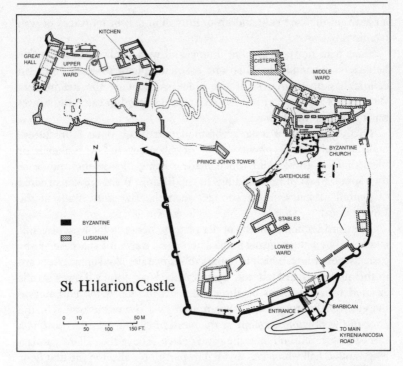

St Hilarion Castle

Lusignan with a semicircular Byzantine arch in the wall above. There is no drawbridge or portcullis but above the wooden door are the four brackets of a machicoulis, a parapet with openings between supporting corbels for dropping stones on attackers. One bracket is decorated with a woman's head wearing the horned headdress fashionable in the fifteenth century. Inside the bailey there are several large cisterns against the walls. The only building of note is the stable, with a vaulted roof and a doorway high enough to admit camels.

The Middle Ward, or Main Guard, is more strongly defended and contains the main group of buildings. The original drawbridge has disappeared but the great gatehouse remains leading to a tunnel which gives on to a maze of buildings at different levels. On the right is the Byzantine chapel, probably part of the original monastery, which was preserved and strengthened in the thirteenth century. It is built of thin bricks and mortar with courses of rubble stonework at intervals. The dome, now gone, was supported by eight arches, some of which have recently been reconstructed. This is an unusual plan (seen also at nearby Antiphonitis). The church has a square nave with an apse on the east side and an oratory, and still bears traces of wall painting.

Steps lead down to a large dining hall with kitchens nearby. The belvedere is unique to Hilarion; a square platform with a vaulted ceiling has open arches on two sides overlooking the magnificent view. Nearby is another immense cistern designed to catch the winter rains from the bluff above.

To the north is a long accommodation block once four storeys high. It had a high pitched roof, possibly covered with thatch or tiles (there is an old kiln which made roofing tiles in the middle of the range). Most of the buildings in the Middle Ward are constructed of jointed masonry, much stronger than the Byzantine walls in the Lower Ward.

The third section is on the upper plateau, between the twin peaks. It is reached by a steep zigzag path. There is no trace of a staircase or any easier access route, which is remarkable since the royal apartments are in this upper ward. Half-way up the path, King John's Tower stands isolated with precipices on three sides. At the top is the entrance to the courtyard through a Lusignan arch in a Byzantine wall. On the edge of the precipitous slope at the western end of the courtyard, is a fine two-storeyed building, the royal palace. Above the cellars stands a long vaulted hall which was divided by partition walls. On the first floor are the remains of the upper chambers, with the elegant Gothic tracery of the Queen's Window and, at the north end, a passage leading to a latrine. A wooden gallery ran along the east side and provided access to the chambers. Higher up, a wall with a tower is built along the ridge of the mountain.

St Hilarion is the largest and most complex castle in Cyprus. An invaluable guide published by the Turkish Society of Friends of Antiquities and Museums of Kıbrıs is available at the gatehouse. It provides a detailed step-by-step tour of the castle, illustrated by an excellent numbered plan.

The Castle of Kantara

Kantara, the most easterly of the medieval castles on the Kyrenia range, was originally a Byzantine fortress of the ninth century. The name is of Arabic origin, possibly meaning encampment or bridge. It is perched on a large, isolated pillar of rock, protected on three sides by steep precipices. Although Buffavento is higher, the view from the top of Kantara is unsurpassed. It commands the neck of the

Karpas peninsula and the Bay of Salamis as well as the whole line
of the northern coast and the Taurus mountains on the mainland.

From İskele (Trikomo) take the road north to the village of Kantara. The
castle is about 2 miles (4 km.) past the village.

The chronicles contain few references to Kantara. The first was in
1191 when Isaac Comnenus took refuge in the northern range before
he surrendered to Richard I. He is supposed to have given himself up
on condition he was not put into iron fetters; Richard, a man of his
word, had some chains specially made of silver.

The castle was rebuilt by the Lusignans in the thirteenth century
when it was known as La Candaire or Cantare. During the war with
the Emperor Frederick II it was twice held by the Imperialists, who
held out for months despite being practically unarmed. After the final
defeat of the Imperialists, it finally surrendered to Philip de Novare
(who always seemed to end up where the action was).

During the Genoese war, Kantara held for the king. John, Prince of
Antioch, was at first held prisoner in Famagusta with his nephew the
young king. He escaped to Kantara with the help of his faithful cook.
The cook disguised John as a kitchen boy, with large boots drawn up
over his leg irons, a copper pot on his head and another in his hand.
He passed the guard by saying he was taking them to be plated with
tin. John later moved from Kantara to St Hilarion and was joined by
his Bulgarian guard. His brother James, who was crowned king on
his return from captivity in Genoa, refortified the castle in 1391. He
appreciated its strategic value as a check on the Genoese who by that
time held Famagusta.

The Venetians garrisoned it until 1525 then abandoned it.

Guide to Kantara

The main gate is on the east side where the cliffs are comparatively
accessible. This is the most imposing part of the castle. The gate is
protected by an outer bailey formed by a ruined wall; on each side
of the entrance stand small round towers with crenellations. Behind
this outer defence is a very high wall, ending in two flanking towers.
The main gate is set at an angle to allow for covering fire from the
towers. Once inside the court, the south-east tower is to the left;
there is a cistern in the cellar. Then come the custodian's lodge, a
range of vaulted rooms and a latrine. Following the south wall, we

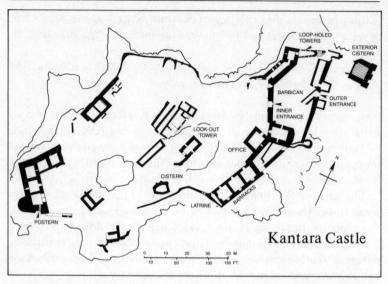

LOOP-HOLED TOWERS
EXTERIOR CISTERN
BARBICAN
OUTER ENTRANCE
INNER ENTRANCE
LOOK-OUT TOWER
OFFICE
CISTERN
BARRACKS
LATRINE
POSTERN

Kantara Castle

0   10   20   30   20 M.
   10   50   100   150 FT.

come to a horseshoe-shaped cistern to store rainwater, and a mass of ruins. In the south-west corner are a tower and another range of vaulted rooms.

The north wall abuts on a steep cliff and has no significant remains. A steep path leads up to the highest point with the ruins of a small building and a fine vaulted window. The most interesting part of the fortifications is the tower which flanks the entrance in the north-east corner. Here a loopholed passage leads to a square vaulted chamber and on to a horseshoe tower extension with seven loopholes to the north, east and south. The upper floor, now ruined, had an upper passage and square room with an opening on to the roof of the extension. This upper terrace was protected by a loopholed parapet. A projecting turret like this is unusual if not unique. It is difficult to explain its purpose, though it does command the main gate and protect the large cistern below it, which is also unusual in being placed outside the defences.

The Castle of Buffavento

Buffavento is the highest of the fortresses along the spine of the Kyrenia mountains and the most inaccessible. Earlier visitors faced a difficult and dangerous two-hour climb from the monastery of Ayios Khrysostomas. Today, a minor road branches off the mountain road from Kyrenia to the airport at the top of the pass to a point near the castle but is still

*only practicable for a four-wheel-drive vehicle. A steep path leads up to the
castle.*

Its high and exposed position justifies its name 'battered by the winds'
and made it the central pivot in the chain of signalling posts from
Kantara through Buffavento to St Hilarion and Nicosia. It also made
it the least attractive as a residence. Buffavento was never more than
a lookout post and a grim political prison.

The castle cannot be accurately dated. There are traces of Byzantine
brickwork on the west wall, but as the architect George Jeffery pointed
out in 1918 these may have been old recycled materials or an old
building technique which survived in this remote corner of the empire.
Isaac Comnenus, self-styled Emperor of Cyprus, left his daughter in
Buffavento for safety, so a fortress existed at that time. When Richard's
army approached, she came out and fell at his feet. The Lusignans
rebuilt it in the fourteenth century; the entrance seems to be about
this period.

Some of its most famous prisoners are documented. John Visconte
was sent there by Peter I when the latter returned to Cyprus showing
the brutal paranoia which marred the end of his reign. The unfortunate
John, a blameless, faithful and popular knight, had been persuaded by
the barons against his better judgement to write to Peter to tell him
of his wife, Eleanor's, infidelity while the king was in Europe. When
Peter arrived back the barons abandoned Visconte to his wrath. He
was chained in a dungeon in Buffavento and starved to death.

During the reign of James I (1382–98), two brothers were held
as political prisoners in Buffavento. One succeeded in bending the
bars at his dungeon window so that he could squeeze through. He
was faced with the precipitious hillside dropping away down to the
monastery. He jumped for a pine tree below him which broke his fall
at the cost of a sprained ankle, rode to Kyrenia and took sanctuary
in a church. He was recaptured and taken back to Buffavento. Both
brothers were beheaded and the heads sent to the king at Nicosia.

Buffavento was slighted by the Venetians who removed most of the
roofs, leaving the remains to wind and weather.

Guide to Buffavento

The castle was never as extensive as St Hilarion or Kantara and today
little remains. There appear to have been a gatehouse and two wards
containing four separate blocks with dungeons beneath. The highest

building seems to have served as a chapel. The walls were constructed from blocks of limestone taken from the surrounding hills. There are traces of marble architraves to some of the windows, which points to a certain refinement of detail. There are the usual cisterns to conserve rainwater.

GOTHIC CHURCHES IN NICOSIA

St Sophia Cathedral (Selimiye Mosque)

This is the earliest and in some ways the finest of the Lusignan churches. The first stone was laid in 1193. It is probable that a small building was ready in 1197 for the coronation of Aimery. Some twelfth-century work is incorporated in the later church.

The plain, dignified plan is based on the early thirteenth-century French cathedrals. It was built in two stages. The earlier section, around 1225, is the eastern end of the church, including the apse, the choir bays and the shallow transepts. The diocese then ran out of money, and the last four bays of the nave and the entrance porch were not begun until 1319. The cathedral was consecrated in 1326, when it presented a splendid and colourful interior, although work was still going on on the magnificent west front. The cathedral was never finished. It was sacked by rioters in 1360, by the Genoese in 1373 and disastrously by the Mamelukes in 1426. The last Mass was said by Francesco Contarini during the Turkish siege of Nicosia, when he urged the doomed congregation to be steadfast. A few days later he and most of his flock were dead, and the Turks had begun the transformation into a mosque.

Guide to St Sophia

The exterior of the cathedral is not as impressive as Famagusta. The flat terraced roofs, the unfinished towers and the minarets undoubtedly detract from the Gothic ideal. Inside, the building is redeemed by the spaciousness of its proportions. The length is not remarkable – 66 m. – but the width of the nave – 21 m. with the aisles – gives the impression it is much larger.

Beginning with the earliest part at the east end, the altar was in the wide apse which includes the nave and both aisles. Within it is a vaulted ambulatory with four granite columns from Salamis. The transepts are very shallow, with small apses on the eastern side

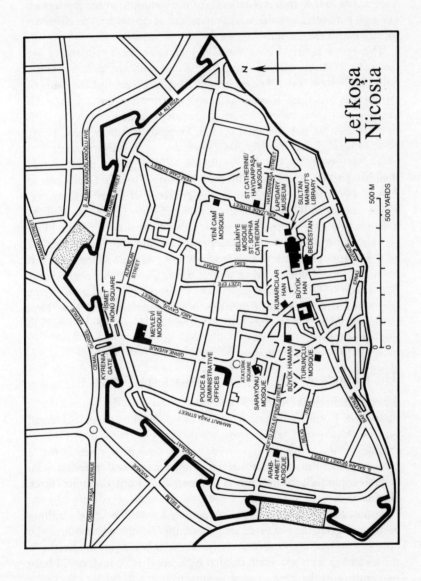

Lefkoşa
Nicosia

covered with semi-domes. They originally held chapels. Today the
mihrab stands in the south transept; in the northern apse, a flight of
stairs leads to the women's gallery. A magnificent marble screen once
cut this part off from the nave but it was removed by the Muslims
together with the carved choir stalls.

The nave is lighted by low windows pierced by the Turks and by the
original clerestory windows which are, unusually, of different sizes.
All stained glass was replaced by white gypsum. Around the walls of
the nave is a curious ledge about ten feet from the ground. At each
vaulting shaft, this gallery descends four steps, goes through the shaft
in an arched tunnel and then up four steps to regain its level. It has
been suggested that it might have given access for maintenance.

In the second bay on the south side a door leads into a chapel
dedicated to St Thomas Aquinas, whose treatise *The Governance of
Princes* was supposedly written for the guidance of a Lusignan prince.
Below the splendid west window with six lights is a narrow gallery,
which would have given an excellent view of coronation ceremonies.

The west front and the great vaulted porch are the most impressive
achievement. The central door is nearly twice as wide as the others. It
has four rows of deep carving; above, where French churches usually
had sculptures, there are panels of white marble which originally
bore paintings. The north doorway is elaborately carved in a floral
design based on the clematis. Small niches in the moulding once held
miniature statues.

The Church of St Catherine (Haydarpaşa Mosque)

This church, built in the fourteenth century, is the second most
important Gothic monument in Nicosia. Outside, large octagonal
buttresses separate tall narrow windows. The west doorway has
marble pillars and a lintel carved with a design of roses between
two dragons; the hood is carved with foliage and finished with
a gabled pinnacle on each side. Above the south door are three
shields.

Inside, a single nave ends in a three-sided apse. The cross-vaulting
is carried on clusters of three small columns. On the north side of the
apse is a beautifully vaulted sacristy. Above it is a room the height of
the church, which was once divided by a wooden floor. It could have
been meant as the base of an unbuilt tower.

On the south side of the apse is a large piscina which drained
through a gargoyle into a small room beyond.

St Catherine has recently been extensively restored and is currently occupied by an art gallery.

The Bedestan

The Bedestan was used by the Turks as a textile market. Under the Venetians, it was the cathedral of the Orthodox archbishop.

It contains the remains of two ruined churches. The northern church, built in the fifteenth century, has a nave with five bays. The fourth bay has a dome, which is round inside and octagonal outside. It is supported on pendentives and pierced by eight windows. The apse has five sides and is vaulted. On the north is an aisle of four bays and an apse with a semi-dome. Altogether a curious mixture of Gothic and Orthodox.

The original thirteenth-century church is immediately to the south. Two aisles remain – the third is under the later nave. The western end is completely ruined. All that is left is a carved doorway that was rescued in 1906 and moved to Government House. The eastern apses remain, carved out of the thickness of the wall.

Facing the cathedral, in the north wall of the Bedestan, are three doorways. The largest has Flamboyant carving and is a degenerate imitation of the great west door across the road. The second appears to be copied from St Catherine's.

GOTHIC CHURCHES IN FAMAGUSTA

The Cathedral of St Nicholas (Lala Mustafa Paşa Mosque)

When the fortunes of Famagusta began to grow after the fall of Acre, the merchants decided to rebuild their small church on a scale more appropriate to a flourishing city. Work began in 1309, after an unfortunate episode when the current bishop embezzled the restoration fund. The building was finished by the middle of the century. It is a rare example of pure early fourteenth-century Gothic, in the contemporary lighter style, marked by larger windows decorated with fine tracery. In use as a mosque since the sixteenth century, it has been spared the renovations and additions which have diluted the medieval Gothic of many European cathedrals. The stained glass windows and the furnishings have gone, leaving the interior a unique architectural experience of pure form.

The Lusignans were crowned Kings of Jerusalem in St Nicholas after their coronation as Kings of Cyprus in Nicosia. At the coronation of Peter II in 1369, a fracas about precedence between the Venetians and the Genoese led to the Genoese invasion and the beginning of the Lusignan downfall.

Guide to St Nicholas

The cathedral is 54 m. long and 22 m. wide. It has a nave and two aisles, all of which end in apses. There is no ambulatory and no transepts. The round columns have plain capitals. The regular clerestory windows have an elaborate arrangement of pointed arches, lancets and foliated circles. The side chapels were added by the Genoese.

Like that of St Sophia in Nicosia, the roof is flat and laid out in terraces. But here there is a wide ledge on the outside of the building instead of the inside gallery.

The church was badly damaged by Turkish cannon in 1571, but fortunately the superb west front survived. Above the three canopied doorways is a balcony, used in coronations. The beautiful west window has six lights and a rose.

The vaulted hall to the south of the porch was probably the chapter house. It is now used for ritual ablutions.

St George of the Greeks

This Orthodox cathedral, built in the fourteenth century when Latin attempts to eliminate the Greek Church had eased up a little, was an attempt to keep up with the Gothic Joneses and out-build St Nicholas. The early Byzantine church was preserved, as was the Orthodox custom, and can be seen tucked under the south wall (cf. the cathedrals of Athens).

The building is one of the largest Orthodox churches anywhere – 39 m. long and 22 m. wide. Byzantine elements are submerged by the Gothic influence of St Nicholas. The central nave and the side aisles all end in semicircular apses in a straight line. They are roofed by half-domes in good condition, and bear traces of mediocre Italianate fifteenth-century paintings. The four panels in the eastern apse illustrate the Descent from the Cross, the Burial of our Lord, the Resurrection and the Women at the Tomb.

Along the base of the walls are tomb niches (cf. St Mamas).

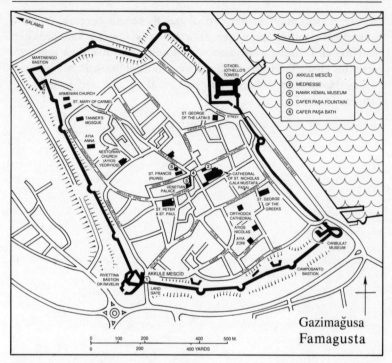

Gazimağusa
Famagusta

Church of SS Peter and Paul

This church is one of the best-preserved in Famagusta, owing partly to its massive construction and partly to being continuously in use since the Turkish conquest. First turned into a mosque, it was later a storehouse and is today a library. It is of rather later date than the cathedrals. It has the usual nave and two aisles, ending in small apses. Here the aisles are lower than the nave, which is supported on the outside by a series of massive flying buttresses, which almost conceal the lancet windows. Another series supports the south aisle. The effect is broodingly heavy.

The best feature is the north doorway, at least a century older, with a gabled canopy and fine foliate carving. A circular turret was once used as a minaret.

The Knights Templar and the Knights Hospitaller

The twin churches are almost opposite the Ottoman baths off the north-west corner of the cathedral square. The Templars' Church, the larger, was built at the end of the thirteenth century. It has a vaulted nave ending in an apse. The belfry is a later addition. When the Knights Templar were dissolved for heresy in 1308, their property, including this church, was handed over to the Hospitallers.

The Hospitallers' church has sockets along the roof to hold the banners of the Knights.

CHAPTER SIX

The Turkish Province

———— o O o ————

THE VENETIANS 1489–1571

When the Venetians ousted the decadent Lusignan dynasty in 1487, they scored the final victory over their old trading rivals, the Genoese. But more importantly they secured a useful naval base for the coming struggle with the Ottoman Empire for the control of the eastern Mediterranean. The fall of Constantinople in 1453 and the capture of Rhodes in 1522 were followed by the Ottoman conquest of Syria and Egypt. Turkey took over the tribute which Cyprus had paid Egypt since 1426 and henceforth regarded the island as an Ottoman fief.

Venetian policy in Cyprus was dictated by the coming showdown. Artillery had made the medieval fortresses obsolete. Now massive ramparts of earth and stone were necessary to withstand the battering of cannon and to provide ramps and platforms for the defenders' guns. So they abandoned and slighted the hill castles, St Hilarion, Buffavento and Kantara, and concentrated on strengthening the ports of Famagusta and Kyrenia, and the capital, Nicosia.

At Kyrenia, they encased the old walls inside new ramparts and bastions, filling the space between with earth. The sea wall they left untouched, as no one had yet worked out how to use cannon on ships. Because Kyrenia eventually surrendered without a fight her walls survive undamaged.

In Nicosia, they built three miles of ditch and wall inside the medieval defences, which were pulled down to give a clear field of fire. The Lusignan palaces and the magnificent abbey were also destroyed. In the 1970s the Venetian wall was strengthened by modern military engineering; along Tanzimat Street it is topped by a line of empty oil drums, pierced by rough peepholes, which gave some protection from the Greek snipers across the ditch.

At Famagusta a massive rampart was constructed along the sea front, completely enclosing the medieval castle known today as Othello's Tower. The Sea Gate, with its original portcullis, was completed in 1496. The Land Gate, or Ravelin, was completed 50 years later. The impressive walls continue along the west side to the splendid Martinengo bastion (named after a famous Venetian soldier), probably the finest example of sixteenth-century military science, which was never taken, even by the Turks.

All this effort was in vain. The art of war was developing so quickly that the Venetian defences were out of date almost as soon as they were finished. And when the Turkish attack came in 1570, no walls could have survived the onslaught without help from outside. Nicosia was taken, and Kyrenia capitulated. Famagusta fell in August 1571 after holding out for a year. When it surrendered, the last Western outpost in the Levant fell to the Ottomans.

OTTOMAN RULE 1571–1878

The loss of Cyprus shocked Europe, but no country was sufficiently moved to send help. The defeat of the Turkish navy at Lepanto in October 1571 was no more than a romantic gesture led by Don John of Austria, the last Crusader. Cyprus was no longer the guardian of the gateway to eastern wealth. Western Europe controlled the new sea routes opened by the explorers. Stripped of economic importance, Cyprus was abandoned to 300 years of obscurity as a minor Turkish dependency.

In 1571 the Turks were welcomed by the Greek-speaking, Orthodox Cypriots, on the principle that practically anybody was better than the Venetians. The Turks, more tolerant than the Latins, justified their welcome by introducing two immediate reforms. They reinstated the Orthodox Church as the official religion, reviving the archbishopric and restoring church property. And they abolished feudalism, allowing the peasants to own their lands outright for a small payment. Taxation was initially reduced. Turkish farmers and craftsmen from the mainland were encouraged to settle on land which had been abandoned under the harsh Venetian regime. It is estimated about 20,000 eventually came over to form the basis of the present Turkish population.

These benefits were unfortunately soon tempered by the misery caused by the inefficiency of the Turkish administration. Tax-collection was farmed out to the highest bidder, who naturally maximized his profits. The Ottomans ruled their ramshackle empire under the *millet* system, which classified their subjects not by race or language but by religion; religious leaders were the spokesmen for their flocks. In Cyprus, the archbishop became the effective ruler by the eighteenth century, working with the Turkish governor for their mutual benefit. Earthquakes, locusts, drought, plague and famine helped to depopulate the unfortunate island. The bishops lost their political power after the Greek War of Independence in 1821. In 1838 the reforming Sultan Mahmut II issued a *ferman* which would have removed most of the administrative abuses. Although most of the reforms remained a dead letter, conditions did improve in the nineteenth century.

The Turks conquered Cyprus at a time when Ottoman classic architecture was at its height under the great architect Sinan. His masterpiece, the Suleymaniye Mosque, was finished in 1557 and was followed by more great imperial mosques in the classic style. None of this splendour appeared in Cyprus, a remote and unimportant province. On the other hand, Cyprus was spared the excesses of French Baroque which afflicted mainland architecture after 1750. Cypriot Turkish buildings are pleasantly moderate, their appeal compounded of simplicity and good craftsmanship.

They fall into three categories, domestic buildings, mosques and public works.

Domestic Buildings

Most traditional Turkish houses in North Cyprus were built on the Anatolian pattern and show a remarkable similarity in design. Large or small, rich or poor, the basic concept rarely varied.

Anatolian domestic architecture evolved from the tented nomadic communities of the steppes. Each tent was a private, self-contained dwelling unit. Extended families grouped their individual tents around a common central area.

When the nomads migrated to Anatolia and built permanent settlements, the round fabric tents changed to rectangular houses of stone, wood or mudbrick. But the house plan retained strong affinities with the cluster of tents around a central meeting place. The living quarters were based on a large central hall, running right through the house. The rooms were arranged on each side of the hall. There was no connection between the rooms; each had one door opening on to the *sofa*, or central hall.

Islamic social and religious customs encouraged the introverted view of the house as an enclosed environment, especially for women. The exteriors are plain and forbidding, but each house conceals a courtyard or an enclosed garden. The typical Anatolian house had two storeys, with the living rooms on the upper floor. The ground floor was often built on stone arches with few if any windows on the street side, and was used for storage or servant quarters. This original plan was modified by contact with more extrovert cultures. In Cyprus, the lower floor is less of a fortress and often contains living rooms.

Inside the most important room was the central sofa with its *köşk*, the enclosed balcony at the end, usually projecting out over the street. This was a light construction of wood, filled in with rubble and plaster. In contrast to the secretive openings on the ground floor it had large windows on three sides, which gave a good view of the action outside, even when partially obscured by lattices. Seating was built-in under the windows.

The internal arrangement of each room recalled the ancestral tents, where every activity had a specific area, and order and simplicity were essential. Seating was built-in around the walls under the windows, leaving the central area free. In the classic examples, one wall was devoted to cupboards which contained all the clutter of daily living. A wooden shelf ran all round the room at a height of about two metres. This determined the upper limit of doors and the rows of windows, and gave a sense of unity. It also divided the room into an upper and a lower area. The lower half was plain and functional. The floor was earth or plain wood; like the seating, it was covered when necessary by textiles. The upper area was more ornamental, the ceilings being particularly elaborate. They were covered with abstract decoration in wood or plaster; rectangular ceilings were often divided up into large squares, which lend themselves more easily to geometric patterns.

Very few Turkish houses in Cyprus contain, or indeed ever contained, all the classic Ottoman features. But the basic elements can often be found – the central through-hall with the rooms opening off each side, the projecting enclosed balcony and the walled garden.

There are many examples inside the walled city of Famagusta, which has been a Turkish enclave since the Venetians. (Famagusta also has two curious houses built over an arch with a road running underneath the arch. There is a third in Dipkarpaz on the road running down to Ayios Philon – empty and rapidly deteriorating.)

The Department of Antiquities is restoring old houses in the quarters of **Nicosia** around the Arabahmet and Selimiye Mosques. At the bottom of Tanzimat Street a large house with its original

ABOVE In 1191 Richard I of England captured Cyprus while on his way to the Holy Land. The island was sold to Guy de Lusignan as compensation for the loss of the Crown of Jerusalem. The Lusignan regime maintained three castles along the limestone ridge of the Kyrenia mountains. The largest of these was St Hilarion.

BELOW The remains of the tenth-century Byzantine chapel preserved inside St Hilarion.

LEFT Bellapais Abbey was founded in the early years of Lusignan rule by Aimery (ruler from 1194 to 1205). The sarcophagus shown here is Roman.

BELOW On the outside wall of the refectory of the abbey are the coats-of-arms of the Lusignan kings. The lion on the barred background is the family device of the Lusignans; as titular kings of Jerusalem they also carried the bearings of the Holy City: gold crosses on a white background.

RIGHT The strategically sited Kyrenia Castle was particularly important to the Lusignan kings who as alien rulers were constantly threatened with insurrection and invasion. In the interior courtyard are the Venetian barracks (shown on the right); the Lusignan sea-wall has alcoves in the battlements to protect archers.

RIGHT The Lusignan gateway in Kyrenia Castle, showing the Venetian wall on the right.

ABOVE Kantara Castle was originally a ninth-century Byzantine fortress. Commanding the neck of the Karpas peninsula and the Bay of Salamis, the view from the castle is unsurpassed.

LEFT The minaret was added to the small barrel-vaulted Byzantine church at Minareliköy when it was converted into a mosque.

RIGHT Sixty-nine arches remain from the Arif Paşa Aqueduct which probably served a farm near Gaziköy (Aphania).

BELOW The Baldoken shrine in the old Muslim cemetery in upper Kyrenia.

LEFT The Haci Ömer Mosque in Lower Lapta (Lapithos) is a charming example of the classical domed Ottoman mosque. There are only two in Northern Cyprus, the second being the Arabahmet mosque in Nicosia (below).

Houses built over archways with roads running through them are now rare in Cyprus. RIGHT This house in Ereuler Street is one of two in Famagusta. BELOW The house over the archway outside Dipkarpaz (Rizokarpaso) is rapidly becoming derelict.

ABOVE Kyrenia Harbour in 1950 showing the nineteenth-century reconstruction. There are two curved moles from the customs house and from the castle.

LEFT The harbour in 1990. The castle mole has gone and the western arm has been extended past the castle, completely closing the northern entrance. The medieval harbour chain was stretched from the customs house to the circular chain tower.

woodwork has recently been renovated. The Derviş Paşa Mansion in Belig Paşa Street has been restored to its former glory and is open to the public. The ground floor is built of stone, and was used as a service area. The rooms open on to verandas with pointed arches on round pillars which surround a large internal courtyard. Water was supplied from a well with a windlass and a beautifully built masonry cistern complete with low-level tap and run-off channels. The partially restored bathhouse at the back of the court still has the remains of the furnace which heated the water and the niches which held soap and washing bowl and a carved stone bowl. An external staircase above the cistern leads up to a hall with rooms opening off it. The upper storey is built of sun-dried brick, with the exception of the large projecting room which is lath and plaster. The even rows of windows on the upper floor contrast sharply with the three openings which face the street on the ground floor. In the bedroom, above the dividing shelf, the upper windows have ornamental lattices and the ceiling is polished wood inside a moulded wooden cornice. The simple bench seating around the walls is loose covered in fabric. The double doors are panelled and carved.

The *Küçük Mehmet* house on the north side of Selimiye Square is built above the Lusignan archbishop's palace. The medieval part dates from the fourteenth century and the mansion was used as the residence of the Turkish governor in the early nineteenth.

In the small *Museum* at the back of the Bedestan there is an important Ottoman ceiling which has been rescued from some demolished building and installed in these somewhat incongruous surroundings. It is interesting because the rectangular area has been divided by a wooden arch into a square and a narrow rectangle, with different decorative designs. The narrow strip would have covered the service area with the wall of cupboards. This was typical of the classic Anatolian house but is the only example known to the writer in Cyprus.

Lefke, the unspoilt university town on the east coast, is notable for a number of typical Cyprio-Turkish houses. Nekipzade Sokak, the road from the statue of Ataturk into the centre of the town, has several built in the 1920s and 1930s. On Salih Sufi Sokak is a large house with good woodwork. At the other end of the town in Haci Emin Efendi Sokak are two earlier houses. Nebkisade House, with the arched green door and shutters, was built in 1908, and is a fine example of a typical Ottoman town house, with a symmetrical plan, full range of upper-floor windows, projecting *köşk* and enclosed

garden. On the left is an even earlier house, built in 1901. It is raised
on stone arches, with an upper wooden skeleton clad in mud brick.

In the part of **Kyrenia** known as the Turkish Quarter is Yazıcızade
Sokak. Here a Turkish family built a row of houses in the 1940s. One
of them is now a grocery store and has been considerably altered.
But at the back is a rare example of a traditional domestic Turkish
bathhouse, complete in all details. It has a small dome with glass
inserts above plastered walls with a whitewashed arch. There are
two built-in tubs, one shallow with a tap to supply cold water when
needed; the deep sink was filled by a hose from the cold tap. The
water was then heated by an outside wood-burning furnace to provide
steam. This furnace also provided underfloor heating so efficiently
that wooden pattens were needed to protect the feet. An arched
niche holds soap and a wooden stool is provided to rest on. A fluted
receptacle, which recalls the more elaborate version at the Derviş
Paşa Mansion in Nicosia, contained hot and cold water from the
sinks for washing. Outside is a small lobby for cooling off and drinking
a restorative coffee.

The Değirmenlik House

*Değirmenlik is a charming and admirably well-kept village on the southern
slopes of the Kyrenia range, surrounded by olive groves. Turn left off the Lefkoşa
(Nicosia) to Gazimağusa (Famagusta) road at the village of Demirhan.*

In the past Değirmenlik was Kythrea, famous for its copious spring
which supplied the great aqueduct to Salamis and worked a chain of
watermills to grind all the flour for Nicosia. A few years ago the spring
mysteriously dried up. Ten mills were still working in 1957, but there
is only one today.

In the main street a large whitewashed house stands on a platform,
approached by two flights of steps. A plaque between two tall arched
doors commemorates the restoration work of the Department of
Antiquities. Iron barred shutters close two more entrances, one
on each side. Inside is a magnificent example of Cypro-Turkish
vernacular architecture. Three solid whitewashed arches span the
central hall. They support the traditional ceiling of cypress poles laid
side by side, filled in with straw matting. Heavy panelled double doors
open into the store and work rooms on each side. A door at the back
leads into the garden. A long wooden staircase leads to the grand hall
on the upper floor, with its projecting balcony overlooking the street.

A wooden arch marks off the staircase end from the main hall. Here the cypress pole ceiling is lower and the rooms smaller. A door leads down to the garden.

The glory of the house lies in the finely decorated wooden ceilings which cover the main part of the *sofa* and the six rooms leading off. The ceiling of the long hall is divided into squares, each with its own pattern. All the rooms have their own variation on the basic theme of diamonds and chevrons surrounded by heavily moulded and beaded borders. The general effect is a restrained and ordered luxury.

Traditional houses are almost impossible to date in the absence of written records. Their constructional methods do not favour long life. Even in Anatolia there are not many more than a century old. The Değirmenlik House may well be nineteenth century, but that is only a guess.

MOSQUES

There are three kinds of mosque in Cyprus: the converted church, the classic Ottoman dome and the rectangular Cypriot style.

Converted Latin Churches

Immediately after the conquest, the Turks converted the Cathedral of St Nicholas in Famagusta into the Lala Mustafa Paşa Mosque and St Sophia in Nicosia into the Selimiye Mosque. They added minarets to call the faithful to prayer five times a day, mihrabs to focus prayers in the direction of Mecca, mimbers or high pulpits, and enclosed areas for women worshippers. Representational art was removed or whitewashed. Otherwise they left the original structures alone. So some of the finest Latin monuments were kept in repair and saved from the tinkerings of later generations. Today they are some of the purest medieval architecture in existence.

Islam changed the orientation of the church buildings it adopted. Moslems pray facing Mecca, and every mosque has a mihrab, or niche, indicating the direction of the holy city. In Cyprus, this is roughly south-east, which accounts for the diagonal carpets laid across the naves of the converted cathedrals. The main axis of a Christian church is from the west door down the vista of the nave to the altar. Islamic religious architects preferred the short axis across the middle, giving a broad rather than a long space. This sits rather oddly in the Gothic cathedrals, where the entrance is still from the west.

Minareliköy is a small village off the Lefkoşa (Nicosia) to Gazimağusa (Famagusta) road. Turn left at Demirhan immediately after the junction with the Girne (Kyrenia) road.

In Minareliköy, a barrel-vaulted Byzantine church has been made into a mosque. Interestingly, structural changes were made to change the axis. The main entrance is now in the middle of the north wall in one of the niches made by the arcading. The west entrance has been filled in. The mimber, or pulpit, under a baroque arch, and the simple mihrab face the entrance across the width of the room. A cylindrical minaret abuts the north-west corner of the mosque, rising beside tiles of the barrel roof.

The Domed Mosque

This is the classic Ottoman mosque with a large dome over a square ground plan. There are only two examples of the square mosque in North Cyprus, the Arabahmet Mosque in **Nicosia,** and the Haci Ömer Mosque in **Lower Lapta** (Lapithos).

THE ARABAHMET MOSQUE   stands in Müftü Ziya Street to the west of Atatürk Square. It is named after Arap Ahmet Paşa, one of the military leaders in 1571. It was repaired or rebuilt in 1845 and restored in 1955. A medieval church originally occupied the site; a number of fourteenth-century tombstones were incorporated in the stone paving, including Louis de Nores 1369 in full armour and Francesco Cornaro 1390, an early relative of the unfortunate last Lusignan queen. The portico for latecomers has three pointed arches and is topped by three small domes. The main chamber is square. The large dome, 6 m. across, rests on an octagonal drum. Four half-domes fill the corners, alternating with pointed recesses, which are decorated on the outside with zigzag ornament. The architecture shows Byzantine influence; the drum rests on arches with the corners filled in with pendentives, rather than the squinches often favoured by Islamic architects. There is little ornament except on the mihrab and the mimber and the columns which support the women's gallery, all of which are made of marble. The minaret is not free-standing; it is entered from the mosque. In the peaceful courtyard a cypress tree and bushes surround an octagonal water tank which echoes the lines of the dome. There are eight graves, including four high-ranking officials, a scholar and two women.

THE HACİ ÖMER MOSQUE, in **Lower Lapta** (Lapithos), is the second example of the classical Ottoman domed mosque. It is much smaller than Arabahmet, but what it lacks in size it more than makes up in charm, surrounded as it is by the luxuriant vegetation and the streams of Lapta. It is unusual in having no portico. The perfect square stands on a raised platform above the road and a small stream which supplies the necessary water. Each side is divided by piers into three arched niches. The front niches contain the entrance and two barred, shuttered windows. All three have raised stepped patterns in the fine masonry. Above the door is a band of formalized flowers and leaves, repeated on the mimber. As at Arabahmet, the dome stands on an octagonal drum; it is supported by eight piers on the inside walls. The minaret is free-standing and bears the date 1911. There is another date, 1870, on one of the window grilles.

Rectangular Mosques

These seem to be native to Cyprus. They consist basically of one rectangular room with an outside portico. The entrance is in the middle of one long wall, with the mihrab opposite. The roof is supported on arches which span the structure at intervals, which recall traditional domestic ground floors. There are no domes.

THE SEYİT MEHMET AĞA MOSQUE, in **Upper Lapta** (Lapithos), is a typical example. The portico has three arches in front and one on each side, separated by columns bearing a wooden roof. The entrance is on the north wall with the mihrab and mimber on the opposite wall. Two arches span the width, one on each side of the central axis. The minaret suffered in the troubles in 1974 and has been insensitively restored in reinforced concrete.

Many smaller mosques follow this plan, although there are local variations. The *Yeni Cami Mosque* in **Nicosia** north of the cathedral was built to replace a mosque converted from a Latin church in 1571. Only the ruined turret staircase remains from the earlier building which was torn down by the governor about 1740 in an unsuccessful search for treasure. The old minaret, built on to the church, was taken down in 1979 because it was unsafe. The plan is unusual in that the portico runs along two sides, the north with four arches and

The Mosques of Lapta

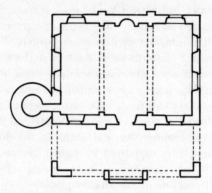

Seyit Mehmet Ağa Mosque (Upper Lapta Mosque)

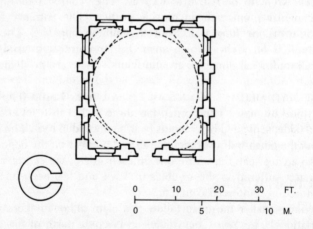

Haci Ömer Mosque (Lower Lapta Mosque)

the west with three. The new minaret was built in 1979. The mosque is the focus for four masonry tombs. Two are attached to the mosque; the domed one holds the marble sarcophagus of the governor who destroyed the original mosque and who was reputedly executed for his impious deed. The other two are across the road. Further down the street is a restored Turkish house.

THE PİRİ PAŞA MOSQUE is the only mosque in Lefke with a minaret. The plan is conventional. The mosque is chiefly remarkable for the grave of Osman Paşa, dated 1839, a superb example of Ottoman carving rare in Cyprus.

THE AĞA CAFER PAŞA MOSQUE, near the castle in Kyrenia, at first seems built on the usual plan, but there are unusual features which indicate it was converted from an earlier building, a house rather than a church. The structure is built above a semi-basement of store rooms, part of which has been converted for ablutions. The original fountain on the other side of the steep street has been partially covered since the road was raised and the steps built. The three arches in front of the portico are carried on squat columns. There is a fascinating plaque outlining the career of Cafer Paşa after whom the mosque is named. He was Captain of the Seas and Governor of Cyprus three times before he died around 1600. He is called 'Frenk Cafer Paşa' which implies he was a European. He began his career as a slave in the household of the Kapudan-i Derya – High Admiral – Kilich Ali Paşa, so he could not have been of Muslim birth. Lowly origins were no obstacle to attaining high rank in the Ottoman Empire. Whoever he was, according to the plaque on the mosque, Cafer Paşa was 'a master of seafaring, an upright and stout-hearted man'.

PUBLIC WORKS

Public works were financed by the state or very often by private individuals as 'pious benefactors'. They include *mescid*s (chapels), *tekke*s (religious hospices), *han*s (caravanserais for merchants), *medresse* (schools), libraries, public baths, aqueducts and fountains for public water supply, and *turbes* (funerary monuments). A lot can be deduced about the ideals and practices of a society by listing its public works. Many were built in Cyprus during the 300 years of Turkish rule. Some deteriorated through neglect, some have succumbed to developers, and some were destroyed in the racial struggles. As most of the surviving examples are in Nicosia and Famagusta, it is convenient to deal with them under these headings.

Public Works in Famagusta

THE AKKULE *MESCİD* has some claim to be the oldest *medresse* in the island. It lies immediately to the left of the modern entrance through the walls; the great arch of the old Land Gate rises on its right. The *mescid* is a classic Ottoman building, rather dwarfed by the massive Venetian wall on which it backs. The exterior is interesting for the carved lozenge patterns which cover the double doors and the wooden window shutters. The two rows of windows are well-proportioned, and set in recessed arches. The water spouts are original. The marble plaque above the door carries a verse from the Koran and the date 1618–19.

THE FAMAGUSTA *MEDRESSE* stands beside the Lala Mustafa Paşa Mosque (St Nicholas Cathedral) in Namık Kemal Square. Originally a theological school, it has been used as a library and recently for commercial purposes. It is basically a large square hall surrounded on two sides by an enclosed gallery. The hall is covered by a decorated dome and the galleries by cross-vaults. The front is divided by four attached piers. The columns between them date from 1489, and were erected by the Venetians, before the *medresse* was built, possibly in the seventeenth century. A side door into the front gallery has a classical multi-arched doorway. Two arched doors open from the galleries into the main hall.

THE NAMIK KEMAL MUSEUM is on the opposite side of the square behind the columned facade which is all that remains of the Venetian Palace.

Namık Kemal was a noted philosopher and poet, whose advanced ideas annoyed the reigning sultan. He was a true idealist, who envisaged not only full democratic rights but a society of nations living in peace under humane laws. He was exiled to Cyprus in 1873 and lived in this small stone building for three years. His grave is in Gallipoli. The cell has a door onto the palace yard. An outside stairway leads to the upper room with a veranda and a marble floor, which is now a museum to Namık Kemal.

In the north-west corner of Namık Kemal Square, to the right of the Venetian facade, is one of the many fountains which still adorn Famagusta, the *Cafer Paşa Fountain*. Turkish fountains were, and often still are, practical sources of fresh water for the inhabitants, not the baroque ornaments of European cities. This one bears an inscription with the date 1597, attributing the fountain to Cafer Paşa, but it is a reconstruction of an earlier fountain which stood in front of the palace. It has a pointed arch forming an alcove which contains a water spout and a trough. The trough is an old marble sarcophagus, possibly from Salamis, like the columns of the adjacent facade. The fountain still functions.

To the right of the fountain, near the scanty ruins of the Church of Saint Francis, is the *Cafer Paşa Bath*. Public baths, with tepid and hot rooms, were an important part of town life under the Ottomans. This is one of the earliest in Cyprus, dating from 1601, and is one of the best-preserved. It was built in the grounds of the Lusignan church; indeed the changing-room is medieval with a cross-vault, and may well have been a part of the earlier building. This is joined by a passage to the small barrel-vaulted tepid room. The rest of the bath, the hot rooms, follows the classic Turkish plan. A large dome inset with circles of glass covers the central area; four halls radiate out, with four private apartments in the corners, each with a small dome. At the back is the vaulted furnace room.

THE CANBULAT SHRINE AND MUSEUM

Immediately inside the dockside entrance to the walled city is the Canbulat Tower (formerly the Arsenal), containing the Canbulat Shrine. The marble sarcophagus is a modern (1968) replacement of the original stone tomb of the Turkish commander Canbulat Bey, who was killed during the Ottoman siege of Famagusta in 1571. The attack on the Arsenal was held up by an ingenious Venetian device, a revolving wheel studded with swords. Canbulat, leading the assault, rode full-tilt at the wheel and immobilized it at the expense of his life. The tower has been made into a small museum.

In the courtyard of the Lala Mustafa Paşa Mosque are two more of the many graves used as shrines.

Public Works in Nicosia

The *MEVLEVÍ DERVÍŞ TEKKE* is immediately inside the Kyrenia Gate, on the left-hand side of Girne Avenue. It was built in the eighteenth century, on land donated by the Lady Emine, who is buried in the garden. The Mevlevi, a Dervish brotherhood, were founded in Anatolia in the thirteenth century and were closely connected with Cyprus from the conquest. In 1592 a member of the sect wrote the history of the events of 1571. Lala Mustafa Paşa, the commander of the 1571 campaign, was a devotee; his copy of the Koran is kept in the *tekke*.

A *tekke* was a religious lodging house; the nearest western equivalent is a monastery. It included a *mescid* or small mosque, shrines, individual cells, kitchens and guest rooms and a communal meeting place or dancing floor: the Dervishes used ritual dances to reed flutes to reach a condition of religious ecstasy.

Like most *tekke*s today only a part of this one is left. Beside the entrance gate is a large pointed arch holding an active fountain. The meeting-house, reached through a yard, is divided into two by arches springing from the central pillars. The first part contains exhibits from the Ethnographic Museum now housed in the lodge. They include Mevlevi costumes and musical instruments. Steps lead down to the wooden dancing floor, protected by railings. A long arched corridor leading out of the meeting house holds the tombs of 16 dervishes; the last died in 1954. Some of the shrines are covered by a row of six domes and some by a barrel roof. Rows of arched windows light the high sarcophagi covered with green cloth and topped by the headgear of the sheiks.

(*For a* Tekke *maintained by another Dervish brotherhood, the Nakşibendi, take the Ercan road out of Lefkoşa (Nicosia), continue straight past the airport turning and take the next road on the right. In 1992 access was blocked by the military*). Near Kırklar is the small ruined *tekke* known as the *Tekke* of the Forty. Forty who, exactly, is not specified but it is a shrine of undoubted sanctity, which was venerated by both Muslims and Christians.

The lodge was built in 1816. The mosque and cells were made of mud brick and are in ruins. But five steps lead down from the remains of the mosque to the underground shrine which was built of stone and has survived. This crypt has three vaulted aisles. The tombs are lined up in the side corridors. Sir Harry Luke counted 23, but was informed that the other 17 were in a mass grave above ground.

The *Hans* in Nicosia

*Han*s are to be found all over the Ottoman Empire, usually in the cities. They offered shelter to travellers, usually merchants, and their animals.

Typically they are vast courtyards surrounded by two-storeyed galleries with accommodation for animals on the ground floor and individual cells above.

THE BÜYÜK HAN OR GREAT INN (between the Saray Hotel and the Selimiye Mosque (St Sophia Cathedral) was built in 1572 by Muzaffer Paşa, the first governor; trade was a high priority after the conquest. It is a fine example of an Anatolian inn. Two entrances lead into the large courtyard. The arcades of pointed arches are carried on columns of round drums with moulded capitals. Sixty-eight rooms open off the galleries. Those on the ground floor were used as stables or store rooms. Two flights of steps on long arches lead to the lodgings on the upper floor. Each cell has an arched doorway, a window opening on the street and a fireplace for cooking. Some of the tall chimneys are original. The Antiquities Department is carrying out extensive repairs, opening blocked windows and rebuilding the stairs and the arches.

In the centre of the courtyard an octagonal domed chapel is raised on marble columns above the noise and confusion. It is reached by an outside flight of steps. Underneath is a square stone fountain provided for ritual ablutions. This *han* is very similar to the Sultan *Han* in Anatolia, which also has a raised *mescid* in the centre of the court. R. A. Jairazbhoy suggests the plan may have been copied from the treasuries in the courtyards of the Syrian mosques, which were domed drums raised on a circle of columns. In the 1950s 60 poor families lived in this *han*.

THE KUMARCILAR HAN nearby is smaller and more utilitarian. The date is uncertain, but could be seventeenth-century. It has been rebuilt and altered extensively. The carved arch inside the entrance passage suggests an earlier medieval structure on the same site.

The inner courtyard, now a garden, is surrounded by upper and lower galleries. The ground floor has low arches carried on square masonry piers; doors lead into cells with stone floors and outside windows. The upper veranda has no arches; drum columns support flat wooden beams which carry the tiled gallery roof. These rooms have marble floors and barrel vaults. Some have fireplaces. The *han* had 52 rooms, now reduced to 44.

THE BÜYÜK HAMAN – The Great Bath – is in İrfan Bey Street (between Atatürk Square and the cathedral near the Büyük Han). It is built on the site of the fourteenth-century Church of Saint George of the Poulains or Half-castes (the Frankish Syrians). The highly decorated Gothic doorway, all that remains of the original church, is now one metre below the raised level of the modern road. In this church, on 17 January 1369, the knights plotted to kill Peter I.

Steep steps lead down to the central changing-room, off which is the tepid room with a dome. Another door leads to the hot room with a large octagonal central stone table. Off this are the four halls and the four domed private rooms. The bath provides the traditional steam bath and massage.

THE BELİG PAŞA STREET BATH   was in use until 1982. It is a small stone building opening off the street. The square changing-room has a wooden ceiling on three arches and is now used as living quarters.

The charming, classical *Sultan Mahmut Library* is behind the Selimiye Mosque. The key may be with the custodian of the Lapidary Museum a little further on. It was built in 1829 by the Governor of Cyprus, in the reign of Mahmut II, the first reforming sultan, who himself donated valuable books to the new library. It consists of one large room covered with a dome, and an annexe with two small domes. Part of the annexe is now the librarian's office. Fine manuscripts and printed books, some rare, are displayed. The interior is decorated with the baroque gilt woodwork of the period.

Fountains

ZAHRA FOUNTAIN   between Zahra Street and Tanzimat Street is an octagonal drum with eight baroque niches containing water spouts, which are still active although the road has been built up around the base. It has an inscription dating it to 1908.

ATATÜRK SQUARE FOUNTAIN   is on the corner of the square in front of the Police Headquarters. It too is octagonal, but with a very elaborate cornice. It no longer supplies water.

SELİMİYE FOUNTAIN   is in the courtyard of the Selimiye Mosque. The trefoil arched niches face the street with spouts which still work.

Public Works in Kyrenia

THE HAZRETİ ÖMER MESCID   stands alone on a desolate seashore about 4 km. east of Kyrenia. A rather vague tradition connects it with the Arab raids of the seventh century. One belief holds that Ömer was an Arab leader who was killed during the raid and is buried here with six followers. It is now a shrine and *mescid* under the guardianship of an iman who welcomes visitors very patiently.

A large covered terrace on the shore is backed by a two-storeyed building which contains the hall with the domed tomb, and living quarters for the iman and visiting pilgrims. The bleakness of the site has been softened by a colour-wash on the exterior and the highly coloured modern prayer mats hung on the inside walls.

THE BALDOKEN SHRINE on the old Muslim cemetery in upper Kyrenia is an attractive domed masonry structure on four solid arches.

THE HASAN KAVIZADE HÜSEYIN EFENDİ FOUNTAIN is across the street from the Cafer Paşa Mosque near the harbour. Because the road now covers the bottom half, it is no longer in use. It has three arches, with an inscription dated 1841 and a badge.

THE KYRENIA CASTLE FOUNTAIN is at the bottom of the hill behind the castle. It is a masonry square, topped by a dome.

THE TAX COLLECTOR'S FOUNTAIN is behind Saint Andrew's Church. It is a vaulted square with a hole on the southern side which collected the water and a spout on the west. It was built by the tax collector after whom it was named.

The Ottomans were always conscious of the importance of good water supplies. In addition to the formal fountains in the towns, minor water installations can still be found in the country villages.

THE ARİF PAŞA AQUEDUCT stretches alongside the old road between Nicosia and Famagusta. *Immediately before entering Ercan Airport, turn left along the old road. The aqueduct is on the left of the road, near Gaziköy (Aphania) village.* The water channel was carried on low pointed arches which follow the road then bend away towards the hills. Sixty-nine arches remain, in quite good condition. The aqueduct appears to have served a farm called Arif Paşa.

THE DOĞANCI CISTERN. *On the Güzelyurt (Morphou) road, one km. before Yeşilyurt (Pendayia) where the government railway turned inland, take the small road on the left marked Doğanci (Elea).* In the small village stands a well-preserved water cistern. The rectangular building has a barrel roof, supported by sturdy ashlar pillars joined by rough stone walling. The overflow shoots are carved stone. The tap is fixed in a niche topped by an old marble lintel. The water was caught in a row of three stone troughs. At the rear a short stone aqueduct leads to the source, now dry.

CHAPTER 7

The British Administration

———— ○ ◯ ○ ————

During the nineteenth century Western Europe showed renewed interest in Turkey as a counter to growing Russian power. In 1869 the opening of the Suez Canal swung the focus back on Cyprus, now a useful strategic base protecting Britain's communications with its eastern empire. In 1878 the sultan leased Cyprus to England in return for a defensive alliance and an annual tribute of £92,800, calculated on the excess of revenue over expenditure for the last four years. Since taxation had been excessive and administrative expenses negligible, this payment proved a heavy drain. The Cyprus tribute never actually reached Constantinople. The British Treasury diverted it to repay part of an international debt on which the Porte had defaulted. This creative accountancy annoyed both the native Cypriots and the British administrators trying to establish a modern infrastructure with the most meagre resources. In 1907 a grant in aid of £50,000, raised in 1927 to £92,800, eased the burden.

The British government administered Cyprus under the suzerainty of the Turks from 1878 to 1914, when Turkey entered the war on the German side, and as a British colony from 1914 to 1960.

The occupation lasted 82 years, exactly as long as the Venetian rule. During this time the British spent more energy and money on public works such as a land survey (under Kitchener), roads, railways and harbours, than on architectural monuments (though Lefke boasts a very small memorial of the coronation of George VI). They were indeed notoriously uninterested even in past glories. George Jeffery, the devoted curator of ancient monuments, had a hard time fighting government attempts to loot ancient stones for road works, and endeavouring to prise money from a niggardly Treasury for essential conservation.

When Jeffery wanted to preserve the ruined tower on Kyrenia harbour which had housed the landward end of the great harbour chain, the only way to interest the administration was to propose converting it into a Customs House (dated 1914). The original square block had been heavily buttressed on the east and west to take the strain of the windlass and was provided with two arrow slits on the east side to overlook the harbour. There was a long one-storey extension to the south and a small round lookout tower, with four arrow slits over the harbour and one, deeply set, looking out to sea. Restoration added a second storey over the main block and a domed roof over the tower. There is now a plan to turn it into a bar for tourists.

A bizarre example of official vandalism is the case of the Kyrenia marble columns. Captain Andrew Scott-Stevenson became district commissioner at Kyrenia in 1880. He was a colourful and forceful personality, notorious for the whip he always carried and occasionally used in the interests of efficiency. In 1883, some ancient marble columns were discovered at the top of Atatürk Caddesi during construction of an inn. There was some reason to believe that they were part of a very early basilica. Commissioner Scott-Stevenson seized the columns after an argument during which he struck the innkeeper, had them carried down to the quay which he was rebuilding, and set them up as bollards. Over the years the harbour road has been gradually built up until only the tops of the columns still stand up among the chairs of the open-air restaurants. Scott-Stevenson was sued by the innkeeper and forced to leave Cyprus.

Public Works

Adjacent to Atatürk Square in Nicosia are the administrative offices and headquarters of the police. Like the less ambitious District Commissioner's Office in Kyrenia, they are built to the Public Works Department (PWD) blueprint for hot climates, instantly recognizable to anyone familiar with former British colonies. Offices are on the first floor to catch any vagrant breeze, wide verandas keep off the sun and through draughts are provided where possible. They offered a working environment in many ways pleasanter than modern concrete blocks, which make no concessions to the climate but rely wholly on air-conditioners and can offer a close approximation to hell when the electricity fails. The old offices had no claims to architectural distinction and made no gestures towards indigenous culture. Solid, unpretentious and eminently practical, they are a not unworthy memorial to British administration and the PWD.

In Kyrenia, the old Ottoman cemetery behind the District Office was a focal point for the British enclave. On one side is the old Country Club, and on the other the *Anglican Church*. This pleasant little building was erected on land given in 1913 by George Houstoun, the first permanent settler to come from England.

The *Country Club* was built in 1932 in the style of an Edwardian villa. The English family who built and ran it originally lived upstairs; the last member left in the early 1960s. By 1990, when the building was in a bad condition, it was rented by the University Sports Club. They raised the money to embark on a programme of restoration and upgrading. The club, now called the Halk Evi University and Sports Club, has been repainted in the original black and cream.

Harbour Works

All districts were allocated some money for public works. In the Kyrenia district, most of the allocation went on improving the harbour between 1886 and 1891. Kyrenia had the only natural inlet along the north coast, but suffered the grave disadvantage of being at the mercy of the prevailing north gales. Two curved moles were constructed from the Customs House and the castle; the western mole ended in a lighthouse. The rock for these jetties was cut by convicts in the quarry to the west of the town, and carried to the moles on a narrow-gauge railway built along the quayside. The new horseshoe shape offered some protection but was heavily criticized by the local fishermen for leaving the harbour still exposed to the north. In the 1950s a new reconstruction extended the lighthouse breakwater past the castle. The eastern mole from the castle was demolished. The northern opening is now completely closed in favour of the new entrance east of the castle.

The Cyprus Government Railway

The Cyprus Government Railway was one of more picturesque examples of a minor transport system. It was built to facilitate the copper trade and to encourage the rehabilitation of Famagusta harbour, which had been more or less moribund under the Ottomans, when trade moved to Larnaca, the home of the foreign consuls and the Levant Company.

A survey for a light railway from Famagusta to Nicosia, combined with the dredging of the port, was undertaken as early as 1878–9,

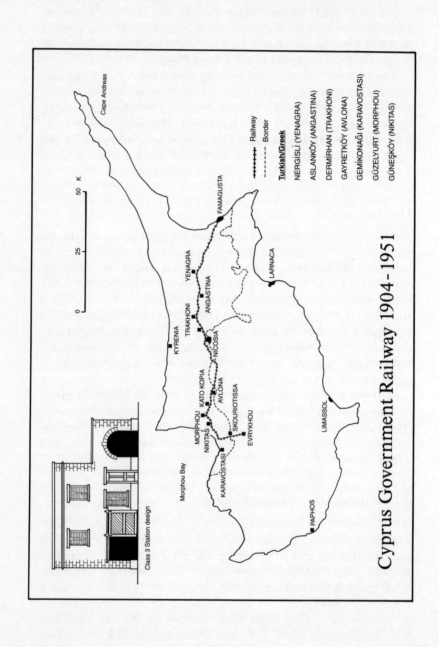

Cyprus Government Railway 1904-1951

Cape Andreas

Morphou Bay

Class 3 Station design

KYRENIA
TRAKHONI
YENAGRA
MORPHOU
KATO KOPIA
ANGASTINA
NICOSIA
NIKITAS
AVLONA
SKOURIOTISSA
KARAVOSTASI
EVRYKHOU
FAMAGUSTA
LARNACA
LIMASSOL
PAPHOS

0   25   50   K

Railway
Border

Turkish/Greek

NERGİSLİ (YENAGRA)
ASLANKÖY (ANGASTINA)
DERMİRHAN (TRAKHONI)
GAYRETKÖY (AVLONA)
GEMİKONAĞI (KARAVOSTASI)
GÜZELYURT (MORPHOU)
GÜNEŞKÖY (NIKITAS)

but there was no money. Twenty years later, the British government agreed in principle and set up a sinking fund to provide finance. In 1903, the Crown Agents sent out an engineer, Shelford, whose report recommended a 2 foot 6 inch track from Famagusta through Nicosia to Gemikonağı (Karavostasi), the copper port, at a cost of £141,526. At the same time the harbour at Famagusta was to be dredged and enlarged. A temporary light railway was built to service the harbour works, which used 'Ruth', a small working locomotive. The three openings made in the city walls at this time were later filled in.

In 1904 Locomotive No 1 arrived. Stations were built along the route on a simple two-storeyed plan with flat roofs, which were later changed to pitched. In 1905 section 1 from Famagusta to Nicosia was officially opened. Section 2 to Güzelyurt (Morphou) was completed in 1907 and Section 3 from Güzelyurt past Yeşilyurt (Pendayia) to Skouriotissa and Evrykhou. The last two places are now under Greek control, as is the section from Gayretköy (Avlona) almost to Nicosia. In all there were 76 miles of track.

In the 1970s much of the track was still in good condition. The railway stations at Nergisli (Yenagra), Aslanköy (Angastina) and Demirhan (Trakhoni) were in use as police stations. Today, the station at Demirhan has been demolished for roadworks; Aslanköy is a military enclave. At Nergisli, the station building itself is a ruin, but the line of the platform is marked by a double row of fine trees. Much of the track can still be traced by this avenue planted along the line; remains of bridges etc. are scattered along the route.

In Güzelyurt, there is a small complex of converted railway buildings. Follow the signs to Lefkoşa (Nicosia) through the labyrinth of town streets. On the outskirts is a large roundabout; take the first road on the left (to Lefkoşa). The railway buildings are immediately on the left.

The office building, now a dwelling house, has had an addition to the first storey and is in good condition. Nearby are the repair and storage sheds, still in commercial use. On the opposite side of the road which has replaced the railway track is another railway building, heavily altered but instantly recognizable by the standard windows, now inside the lean-to shed. There is a large bricked-up arch in the end wall, which suggests this was the booking office (see plan). A short distance down the road the rusting remains of a water tanker and two bitumen spreaders stand at the foot of a high water tower.

Locomotive No 1 was lovingly restored by British army engineers and can be seen in Polat Paşa Bulvari, Famagusta, next to the hospital. Locomotive No 3, rather more dilapidated, is exhibited on the right of the road out of Güzelyurt to Kyrenia; it was built in the USA in 1924.

An extension of the railway served the Cyprus Mines Corporation, an American company which revived the ancient copper workings to become an important factor in the economy of the island from 1923 to the 1970s. There were indications that the ore was running out before the Turkish intervention in 1974, when the Americans abandoned the mines. The main installations can be seen near Soloi, including two long iron piers and a rusting boat.

Domestic Architecture

Cyprus was unusual because it attracted a large number of permanent British residents. They produced a scattering of solid undistinguished villas. One of the most imposing was built by a Judge Advocate in Çamlıbel (Myrtou) in the style of the government offices in Nicosia.

CYPRIOT NEO-GEORGIAN

British occupation began in 1878, at the height of the Victorian Gothic revival in England. But this style never caught on in Cyprus. There are no scaled-down versions of St Pancras Station. Cypriot taste leant rather towards the neo-Classical of the eighteenth century. Georgian and Regency ornamentation was used liberally, even on incongruous mudbrick.

Occasionally one comes across more ambitious examples of what might be called Cypro-Georgian. In the pleasant village of **Değirmenlik (Kythrea),** near the restored Ottoman house (page 106), an imposing and agreeable columned portico adorns a large detached building. Unspoiled **Lefke (Lefka)** is principally remarkable for its fine houses in the Turkish style (page 105). Then suddenly in Atatürk Street one comes across two Georgian facades. The first has a tall doorway flanked by double pillars stretching up to a heavy cornice topped by a triangular pediment. It was built as a cinema. Adjacent is a larger building with three balconies, a similar cornice and a smaller pediment. It was originally a hotel but is now used by Lefke University as a girls' dormitory. Both were built in 1931 by Vasif Bey, the then director of customs. It must have been a fine hotel, with its grand staircase sweeping up between the high rooms, parquet floors (now terrazzo), and panelled wood ceilings. But the external effect is less happy. The neo-Classical details are right but there is nothing of that dignified unity which made the eighteenth-century town terraces so impressive. Builders following an alien tradition often find it is easier to reproduce the formulae than to grasp the spirit which informs the whole. So the flat roofs on the great cathedrals in Famagusta and Nicosia extinguish the soaring effect which was designed to carry the eye upward and was the real inspiration behind all the painstaking Gothic detail.

In **Nicosia** there are happier attempts to naturalize the neo-Classical. Many can be found in what was Victoria Street, now S. Salahi Sevket Sokak. The finest example is the block of houses numbered 71 to 81. These were designed as a unified facade, in the true Regency tradition. The detail includes a solid plinth, pilasters dividing up the facade, string courses and a roof cornice. Impressive doorways are flanked by elegant clusters of Ionic columns. Some original balconies remain. The terrace is unfortunately in a bad state of repair, but it retains its dignity even in decay.

Bibliography

BOOKS PUBLISHED IN ENGLAND

Bitter Lemons Lawrence Durrell 1957. Expatriate view of Cyprus in the 1950s.

Journey into Cyprus Colin Thubron 1975. Travels on foot through the whole island immediately before partition.

The Infidel Sea Oliver Birch 1990. Interesting account of recent travels by an English family in North Cyprus.

Northern Cyprus John and Margaret Goulding 1992. Excellent practical guide, covering everything from transport to natural history.

BOOKS PUBLISHED IN CYPRUS

The Heritage of North Cyprus Rosamond Hanworth 1992. Well researched and beautifully illustrated account of the history and remains of North Cyprus.

Various *Guides* by William Dreghorn. Interesting, though often idiosyncratic, booklets by a long-term resident, with good sketches.

High above Kıbrıs Sonia Halliday and Laura Lushington 1987. Superb aerial photographs of castles and sites. Also *Flowers of Northern Cyprus* 1988.

Historic Cyprus Rupert Gunnis 1936. Republished by Rustem 1973. Description of the churches of Cyprus in the 1930s.

The Enchanted Land Dr Noel Thomas 1985. Personal account illustrating the charm of Cyprus.

The Author acknowledges indebtedness for factual material and interpretation to the following works:

Burch, O. *The Infidel Sea* (Leatherhead, Surrey, 1990)
Catselli, R. *Kyrenia* (Kyrenia Flower Show Edition, 1974)

Cobham, C. D. *Exerpta Cypria* (Cambridge, 1908)
——(trans.) *Mariti's Travels in Cyprus* (Cambridge, 1909)
Des Gagniers, J., and Tran Tam Tinh. *Soloi: Dix campagnes de fouilles (1964–1974)*, vols I and II (Sainte Foy, Quebec, 1985 and 1989)
Dreghorn, W. 'Bays and Beaches', *Cyprus Times*, 1984
——*Famagusta and Salamis* (Nicosia, 1985)
——'Girne Castle', *Cyprus Times*, 1985
Enlart, C. *Gothic Art and the Renaissance in Cyprus*, translated and edited by D. Hunt (London, 1987)
Esin, E. *Turkish Art in Cyprus* (Ankara, 1969)
Francis, R. *Mediaeval Churches of Cyprus* (London, 1949)
Gazioğlu, A. C. *The Turks in Cyprus* (London, 1990)
Gjerstad, E., Lindros, J., Sjöqvist, E., and Westholm, A. *The Swedish Cyprus Expeditions: finds and results of the excavations in Cyprus, 1927–31* (3 vols, Stockholm, 1934–7)
Gunnis, R. *Historic Cyprus* (London, 1936)
Hackett, J. *A History of the Orthodox Church of Cyprus* (London, 1901)
Hanworth, R. *The Heritage of North Cyprus* (North Cyprus Ministry of Tourism, 1993)
Hill, G. F. *History of Cyprus* (4 vols, Cambridge, 1940–52)
Homer, *The Iliad*, translated by W. H. D. Rouse (Edinburgh, 1938)
Hunt, D. and I. (eds). *Caterino Cornaro* (London, 1989)
Ionas, E. 'The Altar at Myrtou-Pighades: a re-examination of its reconstruction', (*Report of the North Cyprus Department of Antiquities*, 1985, pp 137–42)
Jairazbhoy, R. A. *Outline of Islamic Architecture* (Bombay, London and New York, 1972)
Jeffery, G. *Historic Monuments of Cyprus* (Nicosia, 1919)
——*Cyprus under an English King in the 12th century* (London, 1926; reprinted as *Cyprus under Richard I*, London, 1973)
Karageorghis, J. *La Grande Déesse de Chypre* (Lyon, 1977)
Karageorghis, V. *The Cyprus Museum* (catalogue; Nicosia, 1989)
——*Salamis in Cyprus, Homeric, Hellenistic and Roman* (London, 1969)
——*Cyprus from the Stone Age to the Romans* (London, 1982)
Lancaster, O. *Sailing to Byzantium: an architectural companion* (London, 1969)
Luke, H. *Portrait of Cyprus* (London and Nicosia, 1965)
——*Cyprus under the Turks* (London, 1989)
Maier, F. G. 'Factoids in ancient history. The case of fifth-century Cyprus', *Journal of Hellenic Studies*, vol 105, 1985–6, pp 32–9

Megaw, A. H. S. *Byzantine Architecture in Cyprus* (Dumbarton Oaks Papers, no 28, 1974)

Megaw, A. H. S., and Hawkins, E. *The church of Panagia Kanakaria at Lythrankomi, Cyprus, its mosaics and frescoes* (Dumbarton Oaks Studies, no 14, 1977)

Newman, P. *Short History of Cyprus* (London, 1953)

Oberling, P. *The Road to Bellapais. The Turkish Cypriot exodus to Northern Cyprus* (New York, 1982)

Orr, C. W. J. *Cyprus under British Rule* (London, 1918)

Panteli, S. *A New History of Cyprus* (Hounslow, Middlesex, 1984)

Peltenburg, E. (ed). *Early Society in Cyprus* (Edinburgh, 1989)

Runciman, S. *A History of the Crusades* (London, 1971)

Rüstem, K. *North Cyprus Almanack* (Nicosia, 1987)

Sandars, N. K. *The Sea People* (London, 1978)

Schaeffer, C. *Enkomi-Alasia 1* (Paris, 1952)

Stewart, J. R. 'The Tomb of the Seafarer at Karmi in Cyprus', *Opuscula Atheniensia*, vol 4, 1963, pp 197–204

Stylianou, A. and J. *The Painted Churches of Cyprus: treasures of Byzantine art* (London, 1985)

Tatton-Brown, V. (ed). *Cyprus BC: 7000 years of history* (London, 1979)

Taylor, J. du Plat. *Myrtou-Pigadhes: A late Bronze Age sanctuary in Cyprus* (Oxford, 1957)

Tekman, G., Feridun, I., and Bagiskan, T. *Turkish Monuments in Cyprus* (Nicosia, 1987)

Thubron, C. *Journey into Cyprus* (London, 1975)

Turner, B. S. *The Story of the Cyprus Government Railway* (London, 1979)

Glossary

———— ○○○ ————

Agora: public square.

Amphora: large vessels used for storing liquids.

Andesite: acidic volcanic rock.

Apse: semicircular projection at east end of church.

Arcade: line of columns supporting arches.

Architrave: horizontal beams supported by columns.

Ashlar: squared stone blocks.

Astarte: Phoenician fertility goddess.

Atrium: central court of a house *or* forecourt of a basilica.

Basilica: rectangular assembly hall with double colonnade and apse, adapted as plan for early Christian churches.

Catechumena: areas where converts under instruction before baptism could listen to the service. The converts were not allowed into the church itself.

Cenotaph: literally 'empty tomb'; monument commemorating a body lying elsewhere.

Clerestory: upper storey of the nave, pierced with rows of windows.

Cloisonné: enamel inlay in cells formed by thin strips of metal.

Combed ware: pottery decorated by drawing a comb over a thick red slip while still wet.

Corbel: projection from wall to support weight.

Cyclopean: very large blocks of undressed stone.

Dromos: ramp leading down to an underground burial chamber.

Ferman: decree issued by the sultan.

Gymnasium: Greek higher educational establishment.

Hypocaust: Roman underfloor heating.

Iconostasis: screen separating the sanctuary from the nave.

Köşk: enclosed balcony in Ottoman house, often overlooking the street.

Krator: vessel used for mixing wine with water.

Liwan: large building with the entrance opening directly into the ceremonial apartments.

Machicoulis: parapet with openings between supporting corbels for dropping missiles on assailants.

Mangonel: military engine for hurling missiles.

Medresse: Moslem school.

Mescid: small Moslem chapel without a mimbar.

Mihrab: niche in mosque used to show direction of Mecca.

Millet: Turkish administrative system which grouped non-Moslems into 'Nations' according to their religion.

Mimber: pulpit in mosque.

Mosaic: pictures made by joining together minute coloured pieces – usually stone or marble on floors; coloured or gilded glass on walls.

Muktar: village headman.

Narthex: western porch in Orthodox church.

Nave: body of church from west door to chancel, usually separated by pillars from aisles.

Niello: black composition of metallic alloys.

Nymphaeum: Roman shrine dedicated to a fountain or spring.

Obsidian: black volcanic glass.

Opus Sectile: geometric floor pattern made from coloured stones – much larger than the tiny mosaic pieces.

Pendentive: curved triangle between dome and supporting arches.

Peristyle: row of columns around a court.

Pisé: rammed clay, earth and gravel.

Pithoi: large storage jars.

Propylaeum: a platform in front of the burial chamber.

PWD: constructional department of the old Colonial Service.

Quern: hand mill for grinding corn.

Slip: thin coating of clay applied to a pot before firing.

Sofa: central hall on the upper storey of an Ottoman house.

Squinch: structure across angle of square tower to carry a dome.

Stoa: roofed colonnade.

Syllabary: system of writing in which the characters represent syllables, not letters as in an alphabet.

Synthronon: semicircular bank of seating inside the apse.

Tekke: Ottoman religious hospice.

Tholos: round house.

Trébuchet: siege engine for throwing stones, dead horses etc.

Index

———— ◦ ◯ ◦ ————